THE
OTHER AMBLESIDE

by

Barbara Crossley M.Phil.

ISBN 0-9539244-0-8

Typeset and Printed by Titus Wilson & Son, Kendal, Cumbria.

I would like to dedicate this book to
Deborah, Tim and David
without whose support the book would not be written.

I would like to acknowledge my grateful thanks to:
The Ambleside Oral History Group
The Armitt Library
Cumbria Record Office
with acknowledgement to the assistance of the Curwen Archives Trust.

I would also like to thank Alan Hankinson for all his help,
and to David and Anthea Boulton and to Jane and Paul Renouf
for their comments and encouragement.

I offer my grateful thanks to Lynda Powell,
Curator of the Armitt Library and Museum,
and to
John O'Hara and Bernard Wood
who organised the photographic archive at the Armitt Library.

Contents

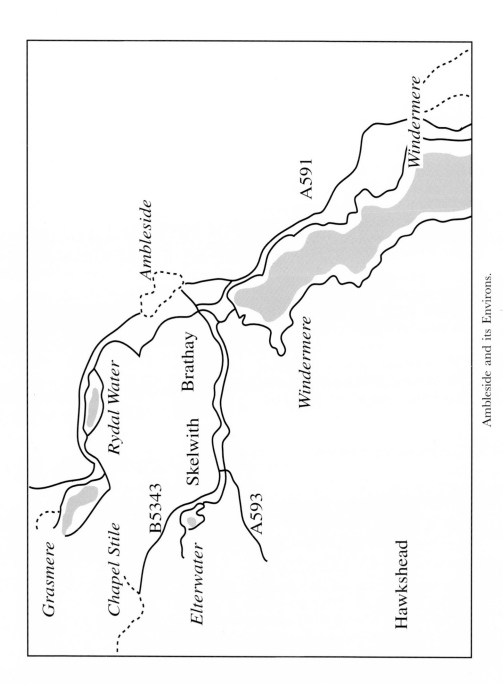

Ambleside and its Environs.

PREFACE

Throughout the period of this history from the 1870s to the 1960s the basic format of the church magazines did not alter. The main function was, and remains, to give all details of all the church services to be held in the forthcoming month. It reflected the pattern of the church year, and it brought to the attention of the reader the importance of the church festivals. It gave details of births, deaths and marriages, of the annual Vestry meetings with the election of the church wardens, it gave details and reports on all church social events, and it acted as a platform from which the vicar could and did proclaim his views and opinions.

From time to time, without explanation, the magazine incorporated material from outside the parish. In January 1880 alongside the magazine a pamphlet called '*Home Words*' was issued, with stories illustrating strong moral imperatives. '*Home Words*' also included articles on, for instance, 'My Next Door Neighbour' and 'The Bright Side of Growing Older'. Later on there were articles on the art of Sir Edwin Landseer, and horror stories of human sacrifice and cannibalism told by Missionaries working in the Niger delta. In 1886, again without explanation, '*Home Words*' ceased.

Initially the Ambleside magazine combined with the neighbouring parish of Brathay; in 1889 Rydal parish was also incorporated only to be dropped in 1902, again without explanation. At this time the magazine cost three halfpence a month and the circulation was 300 copies a month. In 1914 the Hawkshead magazine was incorporated into the joint Ambleside and Brathay magazine.

In 1910 the magazine started to take advertisements and the first one was for cars sold at the Kelsick garage.

Dunlop tyres, motor spirits and oils, Carriages of Every Description done up. John H. Dobson Coach Builder and car salesman.

The magazine was used to raise funds and there was a constant appeal for money for the church. One appeal followed a leak of fumes from the old coke boiler which was so bad the congregation fled gasping from church leaving the vicar in his pulpit somewhat perplexed by the mass exit. Another appeal followed a concert when

the organ recital was marred because the strap connecting the water wheel with the bellows broke in the middle of one piece.

In 1928 Langdale parish was brought in to the consortium, but not for long.

Sawrey parish lasted longer, but in 1934 Ambleside decided to go it alone until 1943 when again links with Rydal were forged. In 1936 the magazine again incorporated '*Home Words*' and included articles on church news in Britain, church artefacts, church music etc. as well as a serial story usually based on the theme of the triumph of virtue over one of the seven deadly sins. It also ran a women's page with tips for washing on Mondays, sewing on Tuesdays, nursing on Wednesdays, cooking on Thursdays, household repairs on Fridays, and childrens matters on Saturdays. This was format was dropped in 1944 when the church took on '*The Sign*', an informative insert from the Diocese.

The vicars of Ambleside through this study are as follows:

The Reverend J. A. Ashton, M.A., 1879-1882
The Reverend Charles Chase, M.A., 1882-1891
The Reverend Bayley, M.A., 1892-1896
The Reverend Pownall M. Lafone 1896-1902
The Reverend J. Hawkesworth, M.A., 1902-1917
The Reverend Bolland 1917-1925
The Reverend Luard Selby 1925-1933
The Reverend H. A. Thompson 1933-1948
The Venerable Wilkinson 1948-1951
The Venerable S. C. Bulley 1951-1959
The Reverend Warren 1959-1967

CHAPTER ONE

'Be Earnest! Be Earnest!'

Introduction

Of all the social changes that have taken place in rural communities from the middle of the 19th century to mid-20th century there are two that are outstanding. The first is in the role of the church and the second is in the role of the state. Taking the first, the influence of the church on parishioners was powerful, and this point is well illustrated in the church magazines where each vicar expressed his opinions on moral issues, some succinctly, others less so. This book is a presentation of the church magazines in Ambleside, starting with the first issue in 1879, which reveal not only the shift in the authority of the church over the period of time, but also reflect the radical social changes that have taken place. There is evidence that the moral authority of the church grew during the 19th century, and was relinquished only after the second world war. The voices of succeeding vicars are important: they were highly educated, dedicated men, often idiosyncratic, autocratic and self-assured, and it is largely, but not wholly, from their point of view this history is written. Although the church magazines provide the core information, supplementary sources are also included, both from the local government archives, and Ambleside oral history archives.

The second point is this; the great reforms to education, to health and housing, to the rise of local government, and to matters concerning industry since the 1870s had enormous impact on Ambleside, and my purpose is to examine how these legislative changes affected both the church and the people. Perhaps this could be seen as macrocosm to microcosm. However, there are many factors affecting any community beyond the control of either church or state. There are the intangible factors relating to loss of faith, as well as the philosophical concepts regarding the role of the state, the great issue being how much should the state intervene, and whether intervention is a force for good or the opposite. Due regard must also be given to the strength or weakness of the economy, to the devastating effect of two world wars, and in the case of Ambleside to the wealth generated by the growth of tourism.

1

The Church

Before looking at the role the church played in the community, I want to place it in the general context not only of the reforms within the church itself that took place, but also in context of the great evangelical movement. After the Napoleonic wars the church was in dire need of reform; there were problems with absentee parsons, with grossly under paid curates and over paid bishops, and there was much dissatisfaction with the power the churches exerted over their parishioners regarding the compulsory church rates. The church did reform the excesses, and evened out to a considerable extent the gross differences in income. Paradoxically as the vicars and curates were given a stipend they could live on, this had a detrimental effect on education which will be discussed later.

Historically part of the remit of the churches was to care for the poor. With the passing of the Poor Law Amendment Act in 1834, power was removed to the Board of Guardians, the poor were removed to the workhouses, and the community was left with the aim of keeping the poor rate as low as possible. According to Owen Chadwick in his book '*The History of the Victorian Church*', Vol 1, the evangelical '*Christian Observer*' newspaper, the '*Unitarian Monthly*', and '*The Morning Chronicle*', warmly supported the Poor Law Amendment Act, whereas '*The Times*' hated it. William Cobbett called it 'the Poor Man's Robbery Act'. Some clergy were in favour of the new Act because they thought the old system 'promoted immorality and encouraged idleness and increased bastardy', whereas others agreed with the principles offered by Adam Smith that all state relief was mistaken since it would both make the poor more improvident and 'the rich would loose incentive to give to the poor'. After the passing of the Act the church continued to ask the congregation to give alms for the poor of the parish, but it did not put up a fight against the state taking the major role. This was in stark contrast to the fight put up by the church later in the century to maintain their role as the educators of the young.

Even though the church might have seemed to have lost ground, they effected one of the greatest social changes in the middle of the 19th century by making Sunday a day apart. At the beginning of the century shops, public houses, markets and fairs were open, and there is no reason to think this was not so in Ambleside. However, the evangelical Lords Day Observance Society became very active mid-century, closing as much commercial activity on the Sabbath as they could, and in Scotland they stopped the trains running.

Owen Chadwick writes:

Lord Shaftesbury, the noblest philanthropist of the nineteenth century . . . who had studied and pronounced on the social evils from child chimney sweeps to the treatment of the insane . . . believed the laws of England should conform to the laws of God and the law of God ordered that no man should work on the Sabbath day.

The church not only changed the role of Sunday, they changed both themselves and the fabric of the churches. Chadwick explained that

> *In 1830 it was a matter of comment if a clergyman could be distinguished from a layman in ordinary life. In 1860 it was a matter for comment if he could not be so distinguished.*

He now dressed in black. If the clergymen lost colour the churches went in for it with decoration, with more fancy altars and altar rails, candlesticks and stained glass. Choirs started wearing surplices, and Holy Communion was given more frequently.

In Owen Chadwick's considered opinion 'throughout the mid-Victorian age the evangelical movement was the strongest force in British life'. Part of the rise of evangelism was manifest with the rise of the Methodist movement which had great appeal with out-door preaching and hearty singing, and, importantly, it embraced the people who felt themselves to be excluded because they were ill-educated. It also led to local rivalries, if not hostilities, between church and chapel.

J. R. H. Moorman in his book '*History of the Church in England*' comments that

> *Mid-Victorian England was fundamentally religious. People went to church and said their prayers and read their bibles. Many families had family prayers every morning with the family sitting or kneeling on one side of the room, and the servants on the other,*

and he goes on to state that the parish church was the centre of village life. 'The Queen led her people on the theme of duty before pleasure', and to her and all the royal family, Sunday was kept as a day apart. In many households on Sundays no serious reading was allowed other than sermons or the bible.

This was the background to Ambleside as it acquired the status of a parish when the new church of St Mary's, designed by the architect Gilbert Scott, was consecrated in 1854. There had been a chapel in Ambleside since 1597, but it was no longer large enough, nor was it near the new centre of the township. When the chapel of St Anne's was rebuilt in 1812 the population of Ambleside was only 624. By the time St Mary's was built the population in the census of 1851 had grown to 1,592. The Reverend Chase who became vicar in 1882, and who enjoyed local history, wrote that he knew

> *of an old circular that was written stating that the new church will contain 940 sittings of which at least 400 will be free. In the event a church of less than half that size was built.*

The majority of pews at this time entailed an annual rent. Mr Chase thought the total cost of building this huge church would be 'about £5,000', and he recognised that the reason for building on this scale was more to meet the needs of the numerous summer visitors than to meet the needs of the resident inhabitants. When the church was completed a hymn was specially composed for the opening occasion which was on 14th June 1854.

3

Shout Loughrigg from your rugged heights
Rotha lift up your voice
Sing merrily ye mountain streams
And all ye hills rejoice.

Five more verses follow along the same lines.

It must not be thought that all the population of Ambleside were Anglicans. A Wesleyan Methodist chapel opened in 1850 for up to 350 sittings, and it also had a small school; the Catholics also had a sizeable following, and the Society of Friends had its Meeting House. This diversification led to some friction, and Harriet Martineau, author, journalist, and local resident, describes the intolerance shown between people belonging to one sect rather than another, and in her Autobiography writes:

it is a serious matter for a working man to offend his landlord by going to chapel, instead of church, when he may be met by a threat 'if you enter that chapel again I will turn you out of your cottage and you know you can't get another'.

Martineau mentions at another time the

discontent in the parish from a dissenter having been allowed to set foot in the school house . . . the doors must be closed against that person.

That person was none other than herself, when she had been asked by the school mistress to give a talk on 'The Sources of the Nile', and, because she was well known as a dissenter, the vicar forbade her to enter into the church school.

A letter was sent from a Congregational Minister on December 9th, 1840 from Ambleside to a member of his previous parish in Salford confirming Miss Martineau's testimony:

In the church here, there has not been for many years, so much as a glimmering of Gospel light, and the place seems to be abandoned as hopeless by all religious denomination. In an apartment of our dwelling, which accommodates about 170 persons, we have conducted religious services which have always been well attended, and we have established a Sunday school which contains 70 children. Our endeavours have all along been much opposed by the neighbouring gentry, and to such extent have their bigotry and intolerance been carried, that they have caused it to be generally understood, that they will deal with no tradesmen, employ no labourer, and bestow charities on no poor persons, who attend our meetings, or allow their children to come to our school. The owner of the house in which we reside has been one of the most determined opponents. He has threatened to sue us for heavy pecuniary penalties, and to eject us from our dwelling. Against all this we have sufficient legal protection, but . . .

The letter goes on to say that he had received support from Ministers in neighbouring towns and he hopes and prays that eventually

'the light of truth may be diffused throughout an extensive and hitherto benighted district'.

4

If there was rivalry for attenders between the church and the non-conformists, as undoubtedly there was, it is somewhat surprising that such feelings or opinions or prejudices were not expressed the magazine.

The church was built to meet the evangelical needs of the times and the size was determined by the growing numbers of visitors. Ambleside in the 18th century was a place of small mills, cloth workers, and farmers, and it was not until the 19th century when moneyed people moved in that Ambleside became a place for tourists. In her Autobiography, Harriet Martineau, in her somewhat breathless prose, illustrated the changes the tourists brought.

Written in 1847 –

coaches run frantically towards us from every point of the compass; a great steam monster ploughs our lake and disgorges multitudes upon the pier; the excursion train brings thousands of the curious and the vulgar; the donkeys in our streets increase and multiply a hundred fold, tottering under the weight of vast females visiting our waterfalls from morn to eve; our hills are darkened by swarms of tourists; we are ruthlessly eyed by painters, and brought into the foreground and background as 'warm tints' or 'bits of repose' . . . the fever lasts from May until October.

The Parson and Whites 'Directory of Cumberland and Westmorland, 1829', was complimentary towards Ambleside,

the town has a modern aspect; the tourists are well catered for at The White Lion Inn and at the Salutation Inn; and industry is well served by a large woollen mill, a corn mill, a tannery, slate quarries and a thriving basket making business.

In the 'Mannex and Co Directory of Westmorland, 1851', it was noted that at the Low Wood Inn

two small cannons are kept at the inn to gratify the curious by the remarkable reverberations of sound.

The time had come to request parish status for Ambleside: both the coming of the railway to Windermere in 1847, and the resultant growth of tourism played their part in this decision. The coming of the railway was opposed by the poet William Wordsworth, who deprecated the

proposal to allow people from the humbler ranks coming to the Lakes because they would not appreciate the romantic scenery, and the Gentry, who settled here, might be driven away,

but welcomed by Harriet Martineau who by her comments on the arrival of the 'curious and the vulgar', seemed to relish the invasion. Perhaps she liked to disagree with Wordsworth:

We have no fear of injury, moral or economical, from the great recent change, the introduction of railways. The morals of rural districts are usually such as cannot well be made worse by any change. Drinking and kindred vices abound wherever, in our day intellectual resources are absent: and nowhere is drunkenness a more prevalent and

5

desperate curse than in the Lake District. Any infusion of the intelligence and varied interests of the towns-people must, it appears, be eminently beneficial . . . considering that mental stimulus and improved education are above everything wanted . . .

Marshall and Walton in their book 'The Lake Counties' endorse the same point that Wordsworth made that up to the coming of the trains

tourism to the Lakes attracted the educated, the élite, the people who concerned themselves with the ambience and the aesthetics.

These visitors would have been influenced by the vogue for the picturesque and the sublime that had a cult following earlier in the century.

It would seem that both groups of visitor came, the vulgar and the aesthetes, and Marshall and Walton make the following points about the effect of the railway on Ambleside. Firstly, with easier transport wealthy people came from Manchester and neighbouring towns to spend the summer by the lake, as it became possible, for the first time, to commute. One of the more famous families to come and eventually settle was Dr Arnold of Rugby, and after Dr Arnold's premature death Mrs Arnold and their children made Ambleside their home. Secondly, these people demanded substantial residences, which in turn stimulated the building trades, and thirdly, by having a second home, this had a beneficial effect both with increase in domestic employment and with the increase in demand for retail goods. Apart from an increasing number of long-stay visitors, the 'resort became accessible to the less prosperous members of the middle class', and eventually 'working class excursions became available'. In any event Ambleside saw a substantial number of new private lodging houses built, as well as more hotels, and 'in 1876 the Ambleside visitor population was estimated at 2,000'.

The church magazine

Twenty-five years after the consecration of St Mary's Church the vicar Reverend Aston decided on 1st January 1879 to start a church magazine in Ambleside.

It has proved a great boon in thousands of English parishes and I doubt not it will prove such in this parish especially as a channel of communication between pastor and people.

The price was fixed at 1/6d per annum for 12 copies, but at Christmas 1879 after the magazine had been going for twelve months, the vicar wrote that they had only been able to sell about 175 copies a month 'which was not enough'.

One of the main messages the vicar wanted to communicate was on the evil of drink.

I am hoping that soon a Branch of the Church of England Temperance Society will be established in Ambleside. I know there is already a very flourishing Band of Hope but there cannot be too much of a good thing.

The magazine reported on a Temperance meeting addressed by the vicar's father, the Reverend J. A. Aston of Cheltenham who gave a lecture on 'Intemperance', when he discussed the ways

> *drink affected not only industry and the prosperity of the people, but also the health of the people. The army suffers enormously from this cause.*

When the Band of Hope was founded in Cornwall in 1847 the message spread rapidly through the land. The idea was first adopted by the Methodists, but many churchmen came to the same view that all alcohol was wicked because it led the way to moral weakness, and therefore total abstinence was the only solution. Congregations began to demand that everyone sign the pledge, and campaigns were mounted for both a cut in the hours public houses were open, and for their closure on Sundays. There were voices raised in the national press that a tax should be put on drink, and there was mounting evidence of a rising incidence of drunkenness, because alcohol was relatively so cheap. In August 1879 in Ambleside a large Band of Hope demonstration was reported in the magazine . . .

> *unfortunately marred by rain . . . but teetotallers are never daunted by water so an imposing procession went through the town . . .*

The small neighbouring village of Brathay shared the same magazine with Ambleside church, and the vicar of Brathay was equally preoccupied with the evils of drink. In August of the same year there was a meeting held in Skelwith school room when farmers were urged to provide non-intoxicating drinks for men in the hayfields . . .

> *a simple and refreshing beverage can be made from a few handfuls of oatmeal mixed with water and flavoured with lemon . . .*

At a Temperance Society meeting at Brathay held later that year it was recorded that

> *although there were only 50 in the audience, on the Parish register it had been noted that there were 70 abstainers and 43 non-abstainers.*

In the general election held April 1880 the congregations were urged to

> *pray before voting, to pray that Public Houses will have to close on Sundays, and to pray that the anti-opium laws were passed.*

Although the working man in the urban areas was given the vote in 1867, it was not until 1885 that the agricultural labourers, and the miners, were enfranchised. A petition drawn up in Ambleside against Sunday opening of Public Houses, prior to the election held in 1880, was signed by 571 people which constituted a significant proportion of the population.

No such Act of Parliament was passed following the general election of 1880, and the vicar of Brathay got up a further petition against Sunday opening of public houses involving the whole community of 97 families. Every family was asked to sign, and the magazine noted that

80 families were in favour of closure, only 2 against, 11 were neutral, and 4 declined to sign.

The vicar of Ambleside wrote:

A Sunday Closing Bill for England is urgently called for. There should be a vast diminution in the number of public houses, we should strive for the reclamation of the fallen, and promote sounder public opinion amongst all classes . . .'.

Harriet Martineau had lectured on Temperance for many years.

When people are compelled to sleep ten, twelve or fourteen in two rooms there can be little hope for their morals or their manners . . . and one of the causes of the excessive intemperance is the discomfort of the crowded dwellings . . . when young men come home to bad smells and no room to turn they go off to the public houses.

Martineau's solution to the problem was to increase the number of houses that had some sanitation and were properly ventilated, and the five or six houses she built – to be bought through a Building Society – were models in that respect.

She lectured frequently using

coloured prints used in Temperance Societies to illustrate the appearance of the progressive disease in the drunkard's stomach from the first faint blush of inflammation to the schirrous condition.

Martineau in her Autobiography noted that she would lecture to an audience 'closely packed', and the talk lasted one hour 20 minutes. She does mention that sometimes men were overcome by the 'illustrations of the drunkard's stomach' and had to leave the room. Martineau wrote about how hard it was to lecture when she was so deaf, and she had to devise a plan to have a 'servant at the end of the hall to wave a white handkerchief if she could not hear'.

Harriet Martineau saw drink as the greatest social problem although she conceded lack of sanitation to be a contributory factor. In a much quoted letter to Lord Morpeth written in 1848, she described Ambleside as a town that is

an abomination in all sanitary respects. The people live in stinking holes; scrofula and consumption abound; whole families are huddled together in single rooms . . .

Martineau then proceeds to make the astonishing comment that 'we have no pauperism except through sottishness'. She did not see what there was to see because her mind was made up that the only reasons for such dreadful squalor were drink and fecklessness.

Health matters were of concern to the church, but the poor housing conditions, the 'stinking holes', did not warrant mention in the magazine. The philosophy of the times was well expressed by Samuel Smiles, who wrote in 1859:

heaven helps those who help themselves is a well tried maxim . . . the spirit of self-

help is the root of all genuine growth in the individual . . . help from without is often enfeebling in its effects, but help from within invariably invigorates.

The onus therefore, was on the tenant to better himself, and by his own effort move to a more salubrious district.

Exhortation and education were the key to improved health. Major Duncan of the St John's Ambulance Brigade asked that

all who can should certainly come to inaugurate a course on what ought to be done and what ought not to be done in cases of drowning, bleeding, apoplexy, poisons etc.,

and in March 1881 a course of lectures were advertised in the church magazine on the subject of health:

'*Food and Health*' by Dr Page
'*Air and Health*' by Canon Rawnsley
'*Water and Health*' by G Tennant, M.B.
'*Health and Morals*' by the Vicar the Reverend J. A. Aston

Perhaps as a follow up to the four lectures the Trustees of Ambleside Charity stated in the magazine that they were prepared to receive applications for help from 'sick poor persons resident in the Township . . . for Medical Attendance, Medicines and Nursing'. The Trustees wanted to make it known that

they only help the deserving . . . applicants must be really sick poor persons. The Trustees are not there to help those who spend upon self-indulgence,

but they did appoint a Miss Campbell 'to act as sick nurse'. The problem for the 'really sick poor persons' would be how to afford her services. The vicar recommended a book to his parishioners called '*Health and How to Preserve it*' at a cost of 1d.

Two years later, when Mr Chase was the vicar, and perhaps because of the amount of sickness among the school children, combined with the prohibitive costs of medical aid, he wrote that he wanted to start a scheme much on the lines of those run by the Friendly Societies with, of course the 'consent of our medical men'. He wanted to form a simple medical insurance club which would involve a fee to be paid monthly and paid in advance. The suggested tariff was for a fee of 5d. per adult and 4d. per child, and if there were more than six in the family the additional members would go free. The system would work in the following way; advice to would-be patients would be given at the doctor's house between the hours of 9 o'clock and 10 o'clock, and if a home visit was requested a 'card' should be left. Patients must be up to date with their payments into the scheme, and 'no change of doctor allowed for one year'. It was also added that 'midwifery, fractures, dislocations and operations' would incur extra costs. The doctors had to have at least 80 names on their lists before they could start the scheme, but two months later in March 1883 the scheme began. Later on the doctors had to modify their charging procedures . . . 'slight accidents were free but broken limbs extra'.

The magazine struck a high moral tone from the first full issue:

Whitsuntide is the season of general holiday making and therefore must be the season of special temptation and danger . . . be on your guard against intemperance, loose language or unseemly behaviour of any kind . . .

Later on in the year the vicar felt he had to comment on the

disorderly conduct on Lake Road on a Sunday evening with . . . gangs shouting . . . using vile language . . . behaving in a vulgar manner . . . residents must control their children and their servants. It might be necessary to form a Watch Committee for the purpose of taking proceedings against these disturbers . . .

Perhaps there was too much levity in Ambleside; in December the vicar published the following verse in the magazine:

Be Earnest! Be earnest! do not trifle.

Life is earnest, when 'tis o'er
Thou returnest never more
Oh! be earnest! death is near;
Thou will perish lingering here.

Be a good Christian example to those around you;
be more earnest in preparing for death and judgment.

The magazine noted births, deaths and marriages, and for some years it continued to announce a birth the following way – 'to the wife of Mr Smith . . . a son' thereby indicating the place women had in this society. Mr Aston was also insistent that parents should bring their children to church personally for baptism and 'not send them'. He was equally firm about Sunday school attendance which, in his opinion was not optional.

Parents must insist on children going to Sunday school. It is quite impossible for teachers when there are truants. The numbers in the Infant Sunday school are very much below what they ought to be, and there are many more children above four years of age who do not come.

The number of church services were increased and Mr Aston wrote:

I am desirous if possible of recommencing soon a weekday evening service at the old church when I trust there will be a good attendance especially of the working classes.

Mr Aston, though only a young man, died very suddenly leaving his widow with small children. His father helped organise the Aston Memorial fund which, as recorded in the magazine raised the amazing 'noble sum of £1,878 11s. 5d.'.

Education in Ambleside

Evangelism was at the centre of the work of the church during the second half of the nineteenth century, and the education of children was a corner stone of evangelism. Historically the church had been the main provider of schools, and many churchmen thought that the main purpose of educating the working classes was to teach the children to read the bible and repeat the catechism. But there were those who shared William Cobbett's comment as quoted by Owen Chadwick:

> *Why should you teach a ploughboy to read and write when these accomplishments would be useless for mounting a carthorse?*

Ambleside had a long history of established reputable schools, and the reason why the education was good in the late eighteenth and early nineteenth centuries was that many ordained priests had to supplement their stipend by teaching. After the church completed the necessary reforms and gave parsons a decent living, many vicars stopped teaching except for giving religious instruction.

The first curate of Ambleside was a school master, John Bell 1585-1634, who served the chapel for 44 years and his name is inscribed in the chapel bible. (This was a first edition of the 1611 translation, restored to St Mary's church in 1906). John Bell not only acted as priest and taught in the school, he also built a causeway in the boggy area between Rydal and Ambleside to enable scholars from Rydal attend his school. Every Thursday and Saturday afternoon he got his pupils to gather stones and help him pave the road.

In 1723 a resident of Ambleside called John Kelsick died leaving property to be used for building and endowing a free school, to be built as near to the chapel as possible. The little school prospered and at one time had a Fellow of Queens College Oxford, the Reverend Isaac King as Headmaster. Mr Dawes, a pupil of Mr King, having been ordained in 1811 as Curate of Ambleside, started his own school and taught both Hartley and Derwent Coleridge. Hartley attended the school for six years and won a scholarship to Oriel College, Oxford. John Wordsworth also attended the school, 'to conquer laziness and shyness' and his younger brother William followed on. The sons of the artist John Harden, then living at Brathay Hall, also attended. The local school was good enough to teach the sons of the local gentry at that time, but during the next decades the public schools gained the support of the middle classes. Dr Arnold had improved the image, many new public schools opened, the new moneyed industrialists wanted their sons to be educated as gentlemen, and the small local schools struggled to survive.

The report of the Charity Commissioners in 1815 gives a good report on the Kelsick school.

> *The School room near the chapel (St Annes' church) built according to the direction of the testator, but there was no dwelling house for the master till within the last two years when one of the principle buildings on the school property was fitted up by the present master, at his own expense, for a residence, and he now lives there . . . The School property consists of between 31 and 32 statute acres of land with several cottages and buildings upon it. The estate is left entirely to the management of the master who has lately laid out considerable sums in improving the property . . . The*

land and houses are let to 16 different tenants at rents amounting to £127 17s. 6d. the school master paying all taxes amounting to £20 per annum. Beside the land let by the master he occupies a field of two statute acres of unproductive bog land. The master has drained it at considerable expense and it is now worth £6 p.a. There is timber provided for school repairs . . . The upper part of the school is used as a granary.

The Master takes all the boys of the township free from any charge. They are taught reading, writing, accounts and the classics. The custom of the school is to set apart Thursday for writing and accounts. Children are not admitted till they can read words of two syllables. Some of the children give a cockpenny at Shrovetide which varies from 1s. to £1. There are not more than half a dozen children who give anything and those are some of the better sort of inhabitants.

There are 30 to 40 boys on average in the school. 14 are learning classics . . . 3-4 young men were ordained in the course of the last three years. There have been 70 boys in the school but many did not belong to Ambleside and the Master now takes no boys but the township.

Although the Kelsick school was not run by the church, it was organised on a religious foundation, and the Headmaster was an ordained priest. Boys, and only boys, obtained an education in the classics which gave them entry to a university.

A flourishing girls' school was also started in about 1807 by a Mrs Dowling and her three daughters, and was attended by Dora Wordsworth. A cousin of the poet, one Dorothy Wordsworth, referred to in the family as middle Dolly, also became a pupil. She became Mrs Benson Harrison, a very influential lady in the town, living at Scale How, the house which is now part of St Martin's College. Mrs Dowling's school may have continued until about 1845.

Miss Anne Clough started a school in 1852 in Ambleside and ran it for 10 years: her most famous pupil was Mary Arnold, granddaughter of the famous Dr Arnold, and her most original idea was that every girl should learn housework! Miss Clough went on to express her concern about the problems running a school for girls. Because teachers were largely untrained and their salaries low, and mid-century women did not go to work unless they had to for economic reasons, it was hard for both pupils and teachers to reach an acceptable academic standard.

The position of the teacher is often painful as they are poor themselves struggling for subsistence . . . schools can be very small with perhaps 12 to 20 children from the ages of 6 to 16 . . . parents often object to the extra expense regarding the purchase of books.

In her school Miss Clough had between 20 and 30 pupils, mostly girls, and she employed two resident teachers. The subjects on the curriculum were Arithmetic, English and Geography: Music and French were taught by masters from outside the school. The fees were 30/- per quarter for each pupil, and the impression given is the school struggled financially. However, although Miss

Clough left Ambleside in 1862 the school was still in existence at the turn of the century. Miss Clough left Ambleside for Cambridge where in a very modest way she started Newnham College which began in 1871 with five students, and became fully inaugurated into the University in 1880; many of the young ladies were to become teachers.

Miss Clough wrote a paper on Middle Class Education in 1866 for the Schools Inquiry Commissioners, and in it she wrote that:

> *parents do not like charity schools and they are willing to pay . . . the gentry and the clergy do not help this class as they are concerned with the really poor – besides in this class are Dissenters, and they on the whole are very independent about their children.*

Ambleside not only had a free endowed school for boys, and fee paying schools, but it also had a National School for Girls and Infants. The National Schools, as they came to be called, were started in 1811 as the

> *National Society for Promoting the Education of the Children of the Poor in the Principles of the Established Church,*

and as early as 1833 government grants were given to the schools, and later Inspectors were appointed to see the schools were not too badly conducted. Standards were not high, and the essential aim of the school was that pupils would be able to read the bible and learn the catechism. Sunday School was 'compulsory'. This was not unusual as the many endowed schools of Westmorland all insisted on attendance at Sunday School. The day began and ended with prayers. However, the National Schools were not free, and the children attended because the social pressures were morally compelling.

Harriet Martineau in a letter to Richard Moncton Milnes, written in 1843, said:

> *I am delighted to hear of the money raising you tell me of but the pleasure is much dampened by the thought of the absolute inefficiency of the National Schools. In them the children are kept out of fire and water and vice, pro tem: but the bible jargon – horrible in its ignorance – is almost all they get in any number of years that they may attend.*

Martineau was always a dissenter if not a free thinker. She was born into a Unitarian family, but as she grew older she first became an agnostic, but by the time of her death she was calling herself an atheist. Her views, strongly held, were at variance with the vast majority of the middle classes and could well have led to social ostracism, and it says something for the people of Ambleside that this did not happen.

The Education Act 1870

There were many compelling reasons why the Government of the day decided to reform the nation's education system. The Conservative Government under

Disraeli had instigated a Royal Commission on Endowed Schools in 1864, and Mr D. C. Richmond's report on Westmorland makes interesting comments on the variation in education standards in the townships. Mr Richmond reinforces the point made earlier that education standards were falling rather than rising.

> *To reintroduce classical instruction into the small townships or to make their schools in any sense secondary would be vain for the endowments are small, and the pupils too few and the parents too poor to make such schools self-supporting.*

In Ambleside Miss Clough gave evidence that in her opinion the Kelsick school, that used to have good reports,

> *was now becoming dilapidated, over crowded, and deficient in ventilation. There was no remedy short of a new school house.*

The Girls' and Infants' School had only one room with one teacher.

A further reason for the new Education Act was because of pressure from both the Chartists long standing claim for universal suffrage, and the rise of the Trade Unions: the great Reform Act of 1867 was eventually passed giving the vote to all working men in towns – but agricultural labourers and miners had to wait almost another twenty years before they were given the right to vote. The famous quip that 'now we must educate our masters' proved correct, and when Mr Gladstone was returned to power in 1868, he decided to put Mr W. E. Forster in charge of education reform. Mr Forster, a Quaker, was married to one of Dr Arnold's daughters and had been highly regarded as a reformer.

The 1870 Education Act of Parliament

> *made it a requirement that there should be a public elementary school under State inspection, available in every district.*

However, the Act did not make education compulsory, nor did the voluntary agencies have to provide free education. The Education Act of 1876

> *required every parent to cause his child to receive efficient education in reading, writing and arithmetic and prohibited the employment of children under the age of ten.*

However, although School Boards were created and new schools were built, mainly in the industrial areas, the rural communities largely depended on what was termed the voluntary or church schools. These schools continued to charge their pupils, and attendance continued to be erratic. Marjorie Cruikshank in her book '*Church and State in English Education*' comments that there was a great variation in standards in schools across the country, and some rural schools were poor in every respect.

Although the Education Act of 1870 was hailed as a great breakthrough, in fact it did very little indeed for the inhabitants of an area such as Ambleside where village schools were already in existence. The children of the poor may or may not have been able to go to school – the boys in Ambleside went to a free school, the girls and infants had to pay – but the essential component of the Act was missing: school attendance was not mandatory. As Moorman commented, the point of the Act 'was to fill the gaps by building new schools, and not interfere with the existing schools'. From now on there were two types of school, the 'provided', which were built by and funded by the state, and the 'non-provided'. The 'non-provided' schools were the majority, the bulk of which belonged to the Church of England, but there were Catholic and Nonconformist schools in existence mostly in the new industrial cities. A slightly more rigorous system of inspection was put in place but often the recommendations were ignored. At the time the Education Act was passed it was thought to cost 30s. a year to educate a child, and out of this the Government paid a third, the voluntary societies or churches paid a third and the parents paid a third. This is an interesting statistic, because Miss Clough charged four times that amount at 30/- per quarter, and she admitted that her staff salaries were low. Throughout the debate on the Foster Act there was implacable opposition from the churches against any form of state aid if it was considered that this was going to lead to any form of state interference.

The Kelsick school had become 'dilapidated' as has been mentioned, and the National School needed enlarging. With the opening of the new church it seemed appropriate to the governing bodies of both schools that they should rebuild, and both schools governors were able to procure land adjacent to the church. The Kelsick school was able to rebuild over the new Wordsworth library on Vicarage lane, and was fortunate to receive £200 from Miss Clough towards costs.

But in spite of having new school buildings with presumably better ventilation and better facilities, a constant theme in the church magazine was the plea from the vicar for parents to send their children to school. The Kelsick school for boys at that time had separate management, so the concern of the church was for the education and attendance only of the girls and infants. The vicar blamed 'sickness' for a lot of the absenteeism, and he wrote that a 'large part of the pupil teachers time was spent seeking absent scholars'. At a later date he wrote that 'many infants of the proper age have not yet been sent to school'.

The 1870 Education Act envisaged children attending school for five years, and following the passing of the Act employers were not allowed to employ children under the age of ten. However, less than fifty years before the passing of the Act the history of employment of child labour in Ambleside was documented. The following letter was written to the Chairman of the Select Vestry, on 3rd December 1822 by an employer living in Back Barrow, at the other end of lake Windermere. The letter is requesting leave to obtain pauper children from the Ambleside poorhouse:

I was in want of children to work in our mills here. Since then I have taken a number from parishes in this neighbourhood and could take 6 or 8 from you upon the following terms. As soon as the children begin to attend we allow each 2d. a day . . . in the course of 9 or 12 months they will probably earn from 4 or 5/- per week. Where we employ women they depend totally upon their own exertions from the first: if they are women with families who cannot attend our regular hours we must decline employing them them as their irregular attendance incommodes our arrangements. We are not allowed to take children under 9 years of age. Our hours of attendance are from 6 in the morning to half past seven at night allowing half an hour for breakfast and an hour for dinner.

I am, Sir

Your mo.obdt. Servt., Thos Catterall

Evidence from the oral history archives taken in the first decade of the twentieth century would suggest that some of the poor school attendance record was due to children working.

Although there was no mandatory requirement in the Education Acts of 1870 or 1876 for parents to make their children attend school, unless the children attended and paid their weekly dues, the school would suffer financially. Therefore it is curious to see in the minutes of the Girls' and Infants' National School for 1874, that at a meeting it was agreed that:

In consequence of the very irregular attendance at the Girls and Infants school and the great injury to the education of the children resulting therefrom, it was resolved that the vicar and Lieut.-Col. Watson be authorised to visit the school and to examine the registers and dismiss in their discretion any girl whose attendance is very irregular.

There were financial problems with shortage of books and shortage of maps for geography, and possibly following the managers inspection, shortage of pupils. Perhaps it is not surprising that in 1876 the managers decided that the school fees had to be increased.

Owing to the rise of salaries, and not forgetting the costs of cleaning and fire lighting, and the deficiency in the school funds, Tradesmen and Employers of Labour would in future be asked to pay sixpence per week for one child in school, fourpence for the second, and twopence for the third and others, and that all other parents pay threepence per week for one child, twopence for the second and one penny for the third and others.

The salary of the Headmistress was £60 per annum, and presumably the second mistress was paid less. Both teachers had pupil teachers, who were paid £10 per annum, and it was the duty of the mistresses to instruct their pupil teachers thoroughly in the scriptures. Only the Headmistress was allowed to inflict corporal punishment 'with an instrument previously approved by the Managers', and 'all such beatings had to be recorded in red ink in a log book'.

The 1888 report by the Government Inspectors on Ambleside school was poor; 'the Managers cannot but feel disappointed'. In fact the report on the Infants school was so bad there was suggestion there might be deduction of the grant. The Managers resolved that 'unless there was improvement the Mistress will be sacked'.

Improvement in educational provision for all age groups was being widely discussed, inside and outside of Parliament; it became the decade when decisions had to be made as to who should control the schools. Marjorie Cruickshank states in her opinion that although there had been in effect a dual system in education between the church and the secular authorities since 1870 the matter had not been satisfactorily resolved. Forster aimed

to obtain complete and efficient school provision . . . with the least possible expenditure of public money and the least possible injury to existing efficient schools.

There was to be 'compulsory provision of rate aided schools'; the church expressed its concerns that it would

entail upon the country an enormous expense but − far more dangerous loss than that of money − it would drive out of the field most of those who care for education and oblige the Government to make use solely of official or municipal agency.

School Boards were duly appointed by Town Councils in the municipal areas and by Vestry meetings in the parishes outside the boroughs. Inspectors were to be appointed but their work was to prove almost impossible for a variety of reasons.

After the Education Act of 1870 the old argument continued firstly about whether education should be free, and secondly whether it should be unsectarian in the rate supported schools. The Act was basically a compromise, a half hearted assertion between those who wanted a national system of public elementary schools under the rate aided authorities, and the churches who stood for the right of the various denominations to run their own schools. Many churchmen held the view that religion was the essence of all education, and obviously not only did they did not want to loose control of church schools, they also expressed their dismay at the religious instruction proposed for the secular schools.

The new School Boards could fix the amount of fees charged and they could make attendance compulsory. This posed problems for the poor, and the question was raised whether the Poor Law Guardians should pay the fees. The Poor Law Authority was of course associated with the stigma of pauperism and the workhouse, and therefore to be shunned. To be destitute was not just a personal disaster, there were also implications of moral weakness. It was not until after yet another Royal Commission in 1885 the matter was resolved in 1891, and school attendance became both compulsory and free. The poor school attendance frequently commented upon by the vicars of Ambleside and Brathay could well be due to the parents of the school children involved not having the money, the necessary 3d. per child per week, and equally not wanting the shame of applying to the parish for relief.

By 1883 the Anglican Church Authorities, fearful of loosing control, had raised over £12 million nationally for building and maintaining their schools. The Inspectors had found wide discrepancy in the rural schools where low educational standards prevailed, and this in turn posed problems for the state in giving grants. The Government insisted that as a condition for receiving a grant the voluntary or church schools should match the funding, and in many cases the churches were unable raise as much as the average expenditure as County or Borough Councils spent on education from the rates. Marjorie Cruickshank wrote that the:

> *average expenditure from the rates for each Board school child was 19s 1d. compared with 8s. 7d. which voluntary contributions made available for each child in a denominational school. Money made more money, poverty bred poverty.*

There was no doubt that the church was a poor provider in many instances; the new Board schools had better buildings, better libraries and above all they could pay their staff higher salaries. The church basically feared that by accepting rate aid 'they would have a form of control that would unchurch church schools', This debate went on till after the 1902 Education Act.

In September 1891 the Ambleside school managers expressed dissatisfaction with the heating and ventilation system in place in the relatively new school. They decided to send out an appeal to all householders to 'realise the absolute necessity of supporting our voluntary schools'. Under the 1891 Education Act if a school decided on Voluntary status, the teachers salaries would be paid for from the rates, but all capital cost had to found by the school managers, or the Vestry in the case of church schools. The vicar wrote that:

> *a school rate would mean 3d. in the £ and therefore a householder rated at £40 p.a. would have to pay an extra 10s. per annum.*

At Brathay the vicar gave notice that the managers of Skelwith School had 'decided to avail themselves of the New Education Act and make the school entirely free'. He then went on to note that the 'school would still need subscribers'. This is a very important point because although the salaries of the teachers would in future be funded by the County Education Departments, money was much needed for better provision of books and equipment because unless standards were improved the grants may be lost.

From 1891 when free education became an accomplished fact the Ambleside vicar wrote . . . 'do see your children come to school as regularly as possible'. But in 1892 he noted that school attendance remained poor. It could have been due to a virulent 'flu epidemic of that year when . . . all Ambleside was in mourning'. Although schooling was now free, parents were still urged by the church to save in the School Penny Bank the money they would have spent on education. The fact that education was now free, even if the churches were urging parents to continue to give financial support, made singularly little difference to the poor school attendance.

The Church Magazine

Education was a fundamental part of the work of the church, but evangelism also meant spreading the message of Christianity throughout the world. The theme could be famine in Kurdistan, Armenia or West Persia, or help for the 'Zenana Mission in Africa', or the 'Indian Female Normal Schools', or money to alleviate 'Distress in Ireland', but every week the congregation was asked to give financial support for aid to the Missions. Mr Chase wrote:

> *The estimated population of the world is 1,470 million, and of that the Christians number 415 million, Mahommedans 173 million, Jews 8 million, while the heathen amount to no less than 874 million,*

and that, as he saw it, was the white mans burden and the scale of the task facing the church. In 1890 he wrote in the magazine:

> *Our interest in Foreign Missions is really a true gauge of the power of our church . . . we rejoice to remember that Charles Darwin himself accepted as a conclusive proof of the power of Christianity that he found the natives of Tierra del Fuego clothed and in their right minds sitting at the foot of the Cross, and to his lifes end he remained a constant subscriber to the South American Missionary Society.*

It can be deduced from Mr Chase's somewhat defensive tone that he was aware of the controversy Charles Darwin had provoked and the implications for the church.

It is perhaps worth speculating on whether the writings of Charles Darwin had any impact on a congregation such as would be found in Ambleside. The '*Origin of Species*' was published in 1859 followed by '*The Descent of Man*' in 1871. The work of several eminent geologists, including the scholarship of Adam Sedgwick from Dent, had shown that the world could not have been created in six days. Owen Chadwick thought that

> *by the end of the century a considerable number of clergy had accepted Darwin's theory of evolution.*

Chadwick thought this was not such a shattering concept to the man in the pew who perhaps never really believed in Genesis. The man in the pew would take his lead from the man in the pulpit, and to the vicar the greatest sin was to become an unbeliever.

Mr Chase was concerned to increase the size of the Ambleside congregation, with greater participation from all concerned. To serve this end he planned to publish all hymns for the month ahead so that the congregation could practise them all at home first. He organised a choir of boys and men forty strong, and for the choir treat they all went to Keswick.

The vicar wanted to see greater church attendance especially on Thursday nights. He wrote that he had read about the new 'Salvation Army' and . . .

> *I wish we could infuse a little of their earnestness and heartiness into our services without their eccentricities.*

William Booth started out as a Methodist minister, but working in the east end of London he became convinced the only way to reach to the poor was by a more disciplined approach. Booth began the Salvation Army in 1878; all officers were teetotal, and through his open air meetings, brass bands and music hall songs, he began his self-help campaign for redemption. Perhaps inspired by this example of evangelism, or responding to the competition, the vicar started morning and evening prayers daily in the church, and he wrote that he wanted the congregation to not only be punctual, but to 'behave with greater decorum'.

The vicar was also concerned with the effects of tourism; written in August 1882:

> *There is one request we would make of our visitors and it is this, that they will endeavour so to order their plans as to enable those who minister to their comforts to attend at least one service on a Sunday. The life of the lodging housekeeper and her servant is a toilsome one . . .*

Written later:

> *We live in days of rush and bustle. Business and pleasure necessarily occupy much of our thoughts. In Ambleside during the summer we have special hindrances to the life of quietness . . .*

At Christmas that year, far removed from the days of rush and bustle, the church held a

> *Temperance Tea with a sound and sober speech given . . . Christmas is the time to pay bills . . .*

Leisure pursuits were not entirely neglected, although they could only be recommended on moral grounds, and the vicar was keen for the newly founded cricket club to develop.

> *We are anxious to see the young men take a keener interest in their cricket club. A regular course of this noble game makes a far better manlier man than loafing about the streets of the neighbouring towns and villages doing nothing.*

Eventually he hoped the church could acquire a boat.

The church was keen on promoting village subscription libraries, and a small one opened in Skelwith Bridge, and in Rydal. Library provision in Ambleside was very good indeed: the Ruskin Library, later incorporated into the Armitt Library, had 212 volumes by 1882, and 58 of them were by John Ruskin himself. Eileen Jay, writing 'The Armitt Story', says the object of the Ruskin Library was 'to possess Mr Ruskin's writings and kindred works, and to promote the study of them'. The library was more of a discussion group for reading papers, and 'prospective members had to submit their names and were admitted by ballot at the ensuing committee meeting'. Annual subscriptions were 'five shillings for ordinary members and one guinea for honorary members. When the Armitt library started in 1912 the twenty-five members of the Ruskin Library automatically became Armitt members. The Wordsworth library built under the new Kelsick school for boys, became a meeting place for the new Working Men's Club that had just started. The Mechanics Institute library, which cost 10s. per year to join, had a reading room, a billiards room as well as the library with 391 novels as well as books on biography, history, science and travel.

The vicar was keen to encourage wider literacy when he wrote:

he could only wonder why every working man was not a member of the Ambleside Mechanics Institute, with its good reading room, a billiards table, and a lending library where books can be taken home for the wife to read.

The number of libraries would suggest a highly literate population, and bearing in mind the expense of joining, it would suggest a working population with a high proportion of skilled well paid craftsmen. This must be balanced by the fact that at the other end of the scale there were the poor school attendance records.

In June 1884 the magazine was pleased to announce the inauguration of the Ambleside and Grasmere Fine Art and Industrial Exhibition Society, which was to have an annual exhibition of painting, drawing, sculpture, architectural and decorative design, carving, modelling, needlework, embroidery and lacework. This society flourished for many a decade.

By 1885 the vicar was concerned to widen the role of the church to include alternate leisure activities. The Young Men's Christian Association movement had been successfully started in 1844, and the vicar wrote that he would like to start a branch of the Y.M.C.A. Friendly Society locally. The aims of the Society were to encourage young men

to be honest, pure, sober, avoid swearing, to respect women, to protect the weak, to avoid betting, avoid sneering and to pray daily.

The Y.M.C.A. opened a 'large hall for 400 sittings' in St Mary's' Lane, Ambleside. It had a

small library of about 800 volumes, and the building was to be used for literacy, educational and temperance meetings.

The Girls' Friendly Society, which was founded in 1879, also started a local branch; the aims and objects of the Society was to 'encourage purity of life, dutifulness to parents, faithfulness to employers and thrift'.

Although the tone of the magazine continued to express an upbeat message regarding the evangelical aims of the church there was no getting away from the severe downturn of the British economy. The 1880s were a time of falling industrial output and economic depression, and all parts of the country were affected. The vicar wrote that although

times were hard and many were complaining of a diminished income . . . parishioners must still give their 1d. per week to the church.

In the 1881 census the population in Ambleside was 1,988 so 'if everyone gave 1d per week this would yield almost £8. 10s. per year'. At Christmas 1884 the vicar wrote of the

> dire distress in Sunderland . . . some here are short of work but thousands there are on the verge of starvation.

He wrote that food was being provided for the local children in the schools, but he pleaded for generosity from Ambleside people to give aid to the poor, and a sum of £4. 5s. 6d raised by only 10 donors was immediately sent off.

In spite of hardship the size of the congregation continued to grow, and the Sunday school had a roll of 280 children – 'but no older lads'.

The economic depression affected the parishioners but it also affected the country parson in many ways; there was loss of income from the congregation, and from patronage. Chadwick writes:

> . . . that although the country parson had advantages denied to his predecessors, he had higher standards of reverence, there were more educated people in the population, and his role was assured, but he was depressed. His income ceased to be adequate and fell in real terms. By 1887 there were more than 13,000 parsons and a third of them had less than £200 a year and a half had less than £300 a year.

By the standard of the nonconformist pastors this was adequate, according to Chadwick, but the rural parson was given a big house and expected to keep a gentleman's style of living with servants, and he would hope and expect to be able to send his children away to private boarding schools. The worst sufferers were parsons whose income depended on glebe, rent from farm land, as labourers were leaving the land to migrate to the new towns. The economic downturn meant that whereas land was profitable in the 1830s by the 1880s it was not. However, the real issue became whether the church could only draw recruits from those who had private means, the upper classes, which used to be the case, or if they could sustain the clergy who came from the less well off section of society.

One consequence of the economic depression was an increase in the numbers of people who considered the only solution lay in emigration. In 1886 the vicar wrote that:

> some of our neighbours have left for Canada . . . with the population in England increasing at the rate of 1,000 daily it is absolutely necessary that more should go to those countries where the population is comparatively small . . . the vicar will lend books about the Colonies . . .

There was an exodus from the township; the magazine reported that there were more live births than burials but a large number of young men were leaving to find work elsewhere.

Depression or no the Golden Jubilee of Queen Victoria was celebrated in 1887 in fine style with the Ambleside Choral Society singing the 'Hallelulia

Chorus': there were teas for the school children followed by games and dancing. The band played by the lake, fireworks were let off and beacons lit. 'The ambitious can conclude with a climb at midnight to some mountain peak'. The vicar expressed the 'joy felt in being fellow subjects of so great and good a Queen'.

Meanwhile cooking classes were to be started for 'the hard working poor' on Thursdays in the afternoons from 3-4.30, and again in the evening at 7.30-9 p.m., in the lecture room, admission 3d.

Thirlmere

Manchester in common with many of the new industrial towns had for years had sweeping epidemics of cholera and typhoid due to both the filthy water and inadequate sewerage systems, and a new supply of clean fresh water was essential for the maintenance of public health. Manchester Corporation decided the Lake District could well supply their needs, and after much argument, and some bitter opposition, eventually Parliament agreed that water could be extracted from Thirlmere.

Although Royal Ascent to the Thirlmere Act was passed in 1879 depression in trade delayed the start on building the dam. Apart from the economic downturn in the early 1880s, there were a series of poor harvests and very wet seasons; there were also over 200 owners of strips of land to 'treat' with over way leaves, as well as dealing with the rights of 400 tenant sheep farmers, many of whom scratched a poor living from small stock. In the event the work on the 96 miles of aquaduct taking fresh water to Manchester started in 1886, with 14 miles of tunnels, 37 miles of 'cut and cover' and 45 miles of pipes. The Bishop of Carlisle was opposed to the aquaduct and all its works but he was pleased to note the navvies 'behaved commendably'. Canon Rawnsley, co-founder of the National Trust, was one who initially objected to the scheme but came to the view both that Manchester needed water, and the scheme was not detrimental to the environment. William Wordsworth, the poet's son, maintained his opposition to creating a reservoir. But the concern of the church in Ambleside was for the spiritual needs of the navvies.

According to Ian Tyler in his book '*Thirlmere Mines and the Drowning of the Valley*' –

For months prior to the start of the scheme newspaper advertisements were placed throughout Britain, and labourers, miners, carters, blacksmiths, masons etc came and were taken on on a first come first served basis. Some men walked, or hitched a lift from as far afield as Ireland, Scotland and Sussex. They were a hard working, hard drinking band of men of all ages and all denominations.

The hutment construction was not ready when men came – accommodation consisted of sparse, wooden plank construction like army barracks. The men slept on wooden bunks or palliasses, and the huts were heated by cast iron stoves which were

Transporting section of pipe from Ambleside to Thirlmere for aquaduct.

> *used for cooking as well as for heating and drying. Married quarters were separated often by only a curtain . . .*

by 1886 there were seven hut sites, and

> *there was a workforce of 437 men, in 40 huts, with 244 women and children . . . making 681 bodies in total.*

Sir John James Harwood in his book '*Thirlmere Water Scheme*' wrote:

> *After the commencement of the works the children of the navvies and workmen were found to be wandering about the mountains, and it was manifest that a deplorable condition of things would soon result unless something was done to employ their time. For the purposes of furnishing some education a day school was suggested, a good room built at Legburthwaite, and a qualified teacher engaged by the Committee.*

Of course the premises were also used as a Sunday school as well as for religious services, weekdays as well as Sundays. This room, and one erected at Wythburn, were also used as a reading and recreation room, and it was said that they were

> *liberally supplied with newspapers and periodicals, given by courtesy of the Public Libraries Committee of Manchester Corporation.*

Local traders from the Ambleside district were pleased with the relatively large amounts of money being brought into the area by the wages paid to the navvies, and they drove their carts carrying meat, potatoes, flour etc. over the

Raise to do business. However, in winter when labour was suspended through heavy snowfalls or a severe frost, then special provision had to be made for the navvies and their families. It will be recalled that at that time if a man did not work for whatever the reason he did not get paid. The winter of 1890 was particularly harsh, and Tyler writes that the authorities 'appealed to the Kendal Board of Guardians to ask for assistance'. The Guardians did not impose the system of indoor relief, but gave 'subsistence payments made at the rate of of 10d per day per adult, and 2d per day per child.' The school room was temporarily converted into a soup kitchen, and daily meals given free to everyone. Because of sickness a temporary hospital was established, first in a miners cottage, built for a lead miner working on Helvelyn, and then the hospital was transferred to Legburthwaite Mill, which was owned by a blacksmith. The hospital was supervised by a Miss Pauline and her assistant; both could undertake visits to the sick living in their temporary wooden huts, and money was made available from charity for the necessary expenditure. Classes were held in the hospital, presumably on basic hygiene and health, and Miss Hodgson from Ambleside undertook to see to the mothers meetings. By 1891, as Tyler writes, sickness within the workforce increased because,

the practice of skebeening or selling illicit drink became a problem . . . many hut keepers were supplying the navvies from their illegal stills.

During the building of the aquaduct in the Lake District the church was deeply involved in providing Missions for the navvies and their families; not only did they support the Missions at the Raise and at Wythburn, they opened a hut for 'wives and families' in Grasmere at White Moss Common. It is recorded that on New Years Eve in 1890, at White Moss Common Mission, a tea at 6 o'clock was provided by workers from St Mary's Church, followed by 'songs, readings and recitations'.

Some local Ambleside men joined the navvies because of the high wages paid

It was said that labourers in the bobbin mills earned about 6s. 6d. per week and working for the Thirlmere scheme ensured wages of about 14s. per week.

The Poor Law allowance of 10d per day would translate to about 5s 6d per adult per week, plus an allowance for wife and children: the workers in the bobbin mills were on a bare subsistence wage, but for the unskilled labourers the choice would be between deciding to join the navvy workforce, if fit enough, and possibly working away, or giving consideration to the long term employment prospects.

At the same time that Ambleside Church was supporting the spiritual needs of the Thirlmere navvies, the parish church at Brathay opened a Mission hut at the huge slate quarry at Hodge Close for quarry men and their families. Services were held twice monthly on Sunday afternoons, and the Mission finally closed down in the 1950s.

The navvies moved down into Lancashire, and the Missions fell into

Construction workers taking a break from their labours.

disrepair. The aquaduct was finally opened in September 1894. The Lord Mayor of Manchester said in his address to mark the occasion . . .

> *that during his term of office he had witnessed coming of the electric light supply . . . hydraulic power supply . . . the enterprise of the Manchester Ship Canal . . . and now Thirlmere . . .*

One benefit derived from the 'extraordinary traffic from the Thirlmere contractors' was that Manchester Corporation agreed to pay Ambleside Council £75 per year for four years to compensate for the damage done to the roads. As a consequence of this largesse milestones were put in place.

The Local Board of the District of Ambleside

The time had come for the formation of local government which was financed by the ratepayers. Because this was public money a democratic forum was created to oversee that everything put before the council was properly administered. The first meeting of 'The Local Board of the District of Ambleside' was held on the 1st January 1885 in the Magistrates room, with the Councillors duly elected under the Provisions of the Public Health Act 1875. At the first election there were twenty-five nominations for nine Councillors, and two builders, one livery stable owner, one grocer, two joiners, two gentlemen and one surgeon were duly elected. A Gentleman became the first Chairman. A part-time Medical Officer of Health had already been appointed under the Public Health Act of 1875. The remit of the Council included road surveying, scavenging, inspecting nuisances, drains and sewers, as well as river pollution, and overseeing the gas and water supply. They also dealt with planning applications, and at the first meeting there was application for alteration to the premises occupied by the Bank of Westmorland.

The inspector having reported that the alterations did not contravene any regulations the same were allowed.

Planning applications were considered monthly. Mr Horrax, a local bobbin manufacturer, was diversifying and needed planning permission for an enlarged sewer for his new laundry.

Main sewers existed, but there were constant problems with overflow, and new bye-laws had to come into force to clean up the dirt and the smells. The Inspector was concerned with midden heaps, and reported:

that the midden at Low Fold was not such a nuisance as to warrant removal under Section 49 of the Public Health Act, but the stable and middenstead were undrained and needed draining.

An order was made 'that the contents of the midden be moved not less than once every three months'. New sewer tanks were needed, the new scheme was to 'cost £1,000 exclusive of machinery', and the waste was 'to be treated with lime'. The Council was rightly very concerned at the amount of waste, both solids and liquids tipped into the streams and the river Rothay. Nuisance Inspectors were appointed to work under the Medical Officer of Health who was concerned with all sanitary matters as well as matters relating to the health of school children. This included the power to exclude children who were ill from going to school.

In 1886 the Ambleside fire brigade was started, the fire engine cost £120 complete with lamps and an alarm bell, but it was stated that 'a chimney on fire became an offence that could lead the householder to the Magistrates Court'. The fire brigade had twenty men, uniforms provided, but they only got paid when they were active. The following year the Council employed men to clean the footpaths, remove household refuse, clean earth closets, privies and cess pits, as well as extending inspection to common lodging houses, slaughter houses, and the knackers yards. Hackney carriages, pleasure boats and other vessels, and horses, ponies, mules and asses standing for hire had to be inspected. There was a stand for ten cabs at Waterhead, but the bye laws were very strict about the 'nuisance caused by touting' when the boats arrived. On one occasion the Police reported five drivers for not wearing their licensed Hackney Carriage badges, and one licensed driver was fined for being drunk in charge of a horse and trap. There were also strict regulations regarding on street parking in Ambleside, and drivers were forbidden to leave their carriages unattended. In the Council Minutes the

Inspector was instructed to make enquiries as to the whereabouts of the Ambulance belonging to the Board and to see that it was put and kept in proper repair.

A steam roller was purchased jointly with Windermere and Grasmere at a cost of £650.

One of the first items mentioned in the Council minutes was the proposal by Mr Redmayne that the Old Market Cross be re-erected, and this would be done entirely at Mr Redmayne's expense. Comment was made that the Electric Lighting Company had not yet delivered the promised estimates. Some members of the Council were 'opposed to allowing Windermere and District Electricity Supply Co Ltd a provisional order to supply electricity' on the grounds that the Council should support their local Gas Works. Gas street lighting had been in place for twenty years or so. Permission for an electric power line to be connected was finally approved in 1898, and the first cables were laid in 1901. Meanwhile it was noted that there was a

> *great improvement to have new lamps placed in Compston Road south of Mr Longmires studio and the other at the corner of Mrs Wordsworth's house at the Green.*

The lamp lighter's salary was increased from 6/6d per week to 7/6d; the lamp lighter started work at 5.30 a.m. in winter, and the lamps were to be extinguished at 10 p.m.

In November 1896 proposals were made for the railway to be extended to Ambleside, and a Bill was placed before Parliament. At the preliminary enquiry one leading proponent said 'Ambleside stagnates because there is no railway. It has not the prosperity of Windermere'. Maps were drawn up, and meetings took place with Westmorland County Council to trace the proposed line. The County Council, and Ambleside Urban District Council were enthusiastic and considered the idea to be feasible. The proposed line would go

> *by Orrest, through Applethwaite and Troutbeck, skimming the front of Wansfell and finishing opposite the bobbin mill.*

The industrialists all appear to have been in favour of the railway line which some enthusiasts thought might eventually go on to serve Rydal, Grasmere, Elterwater, and the quarries in Langdale. The biggest employer in Ambleside was Mr Horrax, the bobbin mill owner, who exported bobbins to India and Italy amongst other places. He used 25,000 cubic feet of timber annually, all of which had to be carted from Windermere. Bricks came from Barrow to Lakeside, then by barge to Waterhead, and cost 25s. per 1,000, and it was argued they would be cheaper by rail.

The Elterwater Gunpowder Company sold 1,100 tons per year, and Langdale Slate Co had 'great potential.' Coal for the gas works could be brought by freight train which would save money, and Mr Fell who owned a machine tool factory at Troutbeck Bridge employing 100 people said 'the railway would be of utmost importance'. The farmers were in favour, and the owner of the Queens Hotel, who also ran the the Salutation Inn, and who employed 70 servants in total, was most enthusiastic. He organised a system for visitors to hire a coach and four from his hotels, and it was said he owned 70 horses. In his somewhat optimistic opinion the district had 80,000 visitors a year, and this number would increase with the ease of rail travel. In the opinion of the proponents no less than '7,000 local people would benefit', which would constitute the entire population of all the valleys.

Although Ambleside's population in 1891 was only 1,989, it was by then the centre of the County Court District embracing Windermere, Bowness, Kentmere, Staveley, Applethwaite and Troutbeck. The Revising Barrister held Court in Ambleside for the Petty Sessions division, but serious crime was heard at the Assize Courts. Ambleside also held the Head Post Office for the area. A further reason for having a railway, so it was argued, was to ease congestion on the road: tolls had been abolished in 1887, and there was now an 'immense' amount of traffic consisting of 180 carts, carriages, omnibuses and riders a day! It was thought that tourist excursion trains would pay for the cost of building the railway, and a question was asked at the enquiry –

should the mountains of Westmorland be available to the labouring classes from Lancashire and Yorkshire?

The Ambleside men replied that 'they would derive benefit and it would improve their social and moral status'. Hawkshead also formed a Light Railway Committee and asked the County Council if they would consider a link coming to them, and the Council replied that they were glad to consider the plan.

The reason why the railway plan failed was not so much because of the opposition from the wealthy landowners, though they put up a very strong fight, but because the London and North Western Railway Company refused to back the plan financially, and therefore the local residents would have had to raise the necessary £165,000 by share offer and debenture stock, and this vast sum was unrealistic. This sum included the cost of £6,000 for the station at Ambleside, and £2,000 for the station at Troutbeck.

The landowners were not the only people to protest against the proposed new railway: Mr Robert Somervell from the shores of Windermere wrote a pamphlet against any extension of the railway into the Lake District, and he got John Ruskin to write the preface. Ruskin used much the same arguments that Wordsworth had used in 1844 against the Windermere extension. Ruskin feared both that the district would be spoilt by the arrival of the working class tripper, and that 'the landscape would be vulgarised with monster hotels'.

After what the operatives spend on drink . . . we should teach them to save enough out of their years wage to pay for a chase and pony for a day. . . . all the railroad company can do for them is to open taverns and skittle grounds round Grasmere which will soon then be nothing but a pool of drainage with a beach of broken ginger beer bottles.

Ruskin went on to comment:

on the certainty of the deterioration of moral character in the inhabitants of every district penetrated by a railway. Where there is little moral character to be lost, this argument has small weight.

In the event the Chairman of the Parliamentary Preliminary Enquiry threw the Preamble out on the grounds that he was not satisfied that such a small community could raise that amount of money, and he considered the tourist season too short to depend on for sufficient income. There was after all competition from no less than nine steamers on the lake, as well as from numerous commercial barges. Meanwhile in 1896 the Council received a 'draft of rules relating to motor cars'. By the turn of the century all ideas for a railway line to connect Ambleside to Windermere were dropped, but the Council pondered about the possibility of building an electric tramway instead.

CHAPTER TWO

'Blessed be Drudgery'

The Church Magazine

If the Church of England was booming at the end of the 19th century the Dissenters and the Catholics were also expanding their numbers. The Wesleyan chapel built on Rydal Road in 1850 had become too small, and because of rapidly increasing numbers a new Wesleyan chapel was built at a cost of £3,500. The Catholics who till the turn of the century had a small corrugated iron church on Lake Road for only 100 sittings, opened a preparatory school for boys. Kellys Directory for 1897 wrote that:

> *Shap Cell, St Norberts Home School and Preparatory Home...takes its name from the Abbey of Shap which belonged to the Premonstratension Order by whom this institution was founded. It was erected in 1893 at the total cost of nearly £2,000 and was intended as the nucleus of a future priory, but is at present conducted as a preparatory school for boys and for the novitiates of the priesthood.*

The priory never materialised, and history does not relate as to how long the preparatory school continued, but the Catholic congregation grew, and a fine new church was built.

The Temperance movement continued to grow in importance, and the vicar of Ambleside was honoured to be asked to address the Church of England Temperance Society. He said it was his duty to

> *protest in the strongest manner against all flippancy and joking on the subject of the terrible sin of drunkenness.*

In January 1896 the vicar of Cartmel gave an 'interesting address'; he spoke on the problems of Public House reform. Perhaps the most interesting fact recorded was that he skated all the ten miles up Lake Windermere from Lakeside to Waterhead, no doubt carrying a small suitcase, and he then skated all the ten miles back again.

The vicar expressed self-congratulation both on the increasing size of the congregations, and also on the amount raised nationally by charities: the Hospital Sunday Appeal in London raised £35,900, and of that amount £28,500 was donated to the hospitals by the Church of England. But school attendance could give him no cause for celebration;

in 1897 the Boys school held 170 pupils and the average attendance was a poor 106.
The Girls and Infants school did better; out of a possible 270 the average attendance
was 230.

In May 1897 Brathay church had a grand parish tea to celebrate the Diamond Jubilee, the 60 glorious years of the reign of Queen Victoria. The Council sent a slightly barbed letter of congratulation to the Queen:

Although you have not visited the Lake District during the 60 years of your reign we have been favoured by visits from the Prince and Princess of Wales, and the Duke of Connaught, the German Emperor and other members of the Royal family . . . We earnestly beg that your Majesty may long be spared to reign over us . . .

In the following year as a tribute to the memory of Mr Gladstone, the Dead March was played at the close of evensong, and a 'muffled peal was rung at the time of the funeral'.

In May 1899 a boy from Skelwith School, Frank Bentley, gained a Foundation Scholarship at St Bees Grammar School; he took papers in Arithmetic, Geography, Algebra, History, Euclid and Latin. In all probability the vicar took a hand in coaching the child, but the point was the rarity of the event which warranted the praise in the magazine. The school Diocesan reports from Skelwith were 'excellent', earning the highest grant possible, and the school was 'exempted from annual examinations'.

In December 1899 the vicar upbraided the congregation on two counts; firstly he expressed his strong views on irregular attendance at Communion services, and secondly he complained bitterly about the smallness of the Sunday offertories. 'It is your absolute duty to give more'. In January 1900 the church authorities decreed the collections were to go towards the Boer war funds, but two months later in March the vicar noted another fall in the offertory. At Christmas that year the vicar took as his text '. . . the meaning and truth of the words Blessed be Drudgery'.

No doubt in response to General Booth starting the Salvation Army, the Church of England started the Church Army in 1891, and in March 1901 the Church Lads' Brigade was formed in Ambleside. Queen Victoria died in February 1901, and the Coronation of King Edward 7th was held the following year in June 1902. To mark the occasion the Ambleside Church Lads went to London to the Prince of Wales Coronation Review, involving 'two long night train journeys and one long day'. In 1903 the newly formed Ambleside Lads' Brigade joined the annual camp at Blackpool; there were '2,000 boys packed together in lines of tents along the South Shore'. There was Church parade every day, and absolute discipline was maintained. Boys were allowed to go into the sea when a whistle was blown, and they had to come out of the sea when another whistle went.

Reverend Chase, vicar of Ambleside from 1882 retired, and Reverend Bayley was appointed; he complained very early on in the magazine that his stipend was only '£177 p.a. plus the Easter offertory'. He noted that the vicar of Walney Island had a stipend of only £118 p.a. 'even though the population of the parish had gone up from 400 to nearer 4,000'. When Mr Hawkesworth took the incumbency of St Mary's church in 1902 there were 12 sidesmen, two church wardens, one verger, one organist, one choirmaster, 40 choristers and provision for two priests. At the smaller church of Brathay there were two church wardens, four sidesmen, one organist, one choirmaster, a choir of 38, one verger and one priest. Two months later the vicar wrote that he was considering changing the church lighting to electricity from gas. However, by 1906 he was persuaded that the 'electric light would be too expensive for the church'.

Ambleside celebrates the coronation of Edward VII

The Jubilee for St Mary's church in 1904 was carried out midst a lot of self-congratulation. Two years later the little 'Home of St Anne's, was opened in Ambleside to

> *provide accommodation and a home for 18 little girls who no fault of their own are homeless and destitute. The young girls will attend the church school, and the older ones will train to be domestic servants.*

33

This Home was run by the Church of England Waifs and Strays charity, and every month in the church magazine there were lists of gifts or donations in kind to the Home. Anything was accepted from an orange, a pinafore, some pictures, jam, a goose, 18 cloaks and tam o'shanters, to beef tea and broth.

College Education

In 1892 Charlotte Mason opened her 'House of Education'. Miss Mason, a teacher, had come to join forces with a friend who lived in Ambleside, and she was fortunate to receive the necessary financial backing to start a teacher training establishment. The aim of the school was to teach both children and student teachers, many of who later obtained positions as governesses. The school, or Miss Mason, ran a correspondence course, both choosing the text books, and setting the timetable for parents who 'signed on'. When William Wordsworth's niece Dorothy, later to become Mrs Benson Harrison died, her house called Green Bank came on the market; Charlotte Mason was able to procure it, and it became Scale How, the main college building, as it is today. The 'practising school' for both children and student teachers became the Fairfield School, a college course of two years duration was devised, and by 1896 there were 35 students in training. Charlotte Mason considered teaching to be a Mission

carrying the breath of Life to God's children, going out two and two with the mothers of our children to labour in God's Vineyard.

The students all had to keep nature note books; they also took daily bird walks, or geography walks, or botany walks or even language walks. On Sundays the young ladies attended both Matins and Evensong, but on Sunday afternoon there were to be no walks, and Miss Mason read her thoughts on the Gospels to the students.

Miss Mason founded the Parents National Education Union and it was her wish that the college would become an established part of the national, if still embryonic, teacher training scheme; the college was duly inspected in 1904, but failed to be recognised.

A year later Charlotte Mason wrote:

my general impression is that morality is not to be expected from the uneducated – it seems that intellectual inanition during school life is the cause of the moral defects we deplore,

Miss Mason particularly deplored

a) loose opinions, b) lax principles, c) certain evils in schools, d) want of finality in judgment and decision, e) unworthy or frivolous pursuits in life after leaving school, and f) shirking responsibilities – therefore education is character building and definite religious teaching is essential.

Secondary education was at this time still only for the privileged few; however, in July 1891 a scheme for Technical Instruction in the Principles of

Agriculture had been proposed by the newly formed County Council of Westmorland who would give a small grant towards costs, and the lectures would be in Ambleside. The vicar while applauding the idea, wrote he would have liked to see carpentry introduced as well. It would seem that the lectures were a success because in the following year the local committee formed to promote technical education in Ambleside, announced that not only would they promote courses in Agriculture, but they had obtained the services of a Mr Backmaster from South Kensington who would lecture on Botany, Physiology and Chemistry. The first lecture would be free.

The 1902 Education Act Nationally

The education debate continued; Marjorie Cruikshank writes that although new education authorities, the Counties and County Boroughs had taken over from the School Boards, wide discrepancies between the Voluntary schools and the Council schools remained. Cardinal Vaughan wrote:

we must get rid of the reproach that our schools are charity schools dependent upon casual alms . . . it makes it degrading that teachers salaries hang on success at a parish bazaar . . .

However, any intervention by the Local Authorities had to be resisted if the churches were to keep their autonomy.

In 1900 there were about 14,000 church schools with between two and three million pupils. There was little disagreement that some of these church schools were in need of upgrading, but there was considerable apathy about spending public money. On the one hand there is little doubt that in many rural areas money spent on educating the working class had low priority; employers were not looking for an educated work force. On the other hand existing provision of secondary education was beginning to be recognised as inadequate. T. K. Derry and T. L. Jarman in their book '*The Making of Modern Britain*' make the point that the reason why Britain, who prided herself on being the workshop of the world, was beginning to loose markets to both Germany and the U.S.A. was that both those countries educated their work forces to a higher standard than the British. Both those countrys acted on the belief that industrial and commercial success depended on an educated work force. Overriding the debate as to whether or not more money should be raised by taxation to fund a decent education nationally, was the fact that the Boer War had to be paid for. It would seem provision of secondary education for rural working class children was woefully inadequate, and that many church schools were inferior to the new council schools.

The 1902 Education Act did try to weld the two, the secular and the church schools, into one whole under an elected body. Church school management committees had to have a third of their members from the local Council and a national framework was created. Provision and repair of the school buildings remained the responsibility of the church, but salaries were to be paid at the same rate as those in the Council Schools; no longer were teachers to be considered as 'parish workers', and it was hoped that education standards would go up. The church continued to argue that denominational instruction should be compulsory in the state schools, and there was to be a long war of attrition in the years ahead between the church authorities and the Councils.

The Education Act 1902 in Ambleside

At the first meeting of the Managers of Ambleside National School under the provision of the Education Act of 1902 the vicar, Reverend John Hawkesworth, was elected chairman; there were to be four 'foundation' managers, and two representatives from the Local Authorities. At the first meeting the Managers opened an account with the Bank of Liverpool Ltd, Ambleside Branch, and the County Council supplied a minute book. The Government Grant was given as £303 11s. 6d. for the year. As a consequence of the Inspectors report the Managers 'feel bound to make some enlargement'. His Majesties Inspectors visited annually, and every year they made the same comments that the school must provide better accommodation. The premises were inadequate, but the Managers did nothing about the problem until 1910 when a new Infants school was opened and another 160 places created. The new school, built at the bottom of the boys playground, was erected at the cost of £1,130, which had to be raised by public subscription. The managers were proud to announce that 'there is a marching corridor in the centre of the building with class rooms on either side, with cloak rooms, lavatories etc.'.

Although the school Managers did not manage to fund the new infants department for eight years after the Education Act, they were aware of the inadequacy of the local educational provision. The vicar attended an Ambleside Council meeting and made quite a radical suggestion when he said

> that the local elementary school should be condemned as insufficient for the number of children attending,

and he wanted a plan submitted for funds from the Kelsick charity to provide secondary education for all children between the ages of 12 and 16, with no fees for the first two years, and 6d per week thereafter. He did not stipulate if the school leaving age should be raised from the current leaving age of twelve.

A further concession to non-Anglicans was incorporated into the 1902 Education Act, by allowing parents to remove their children from the scripture lessons and religious instruction given in church schools if they conscientiously objected. In 1903 the Managers of the Ambleside school received the following letter:

> As Roman Catholic Priest and with personal anxiety about the religious education of the poor children whose parents are bound in conscience to withdraw them from religious instruction other than that consummate with their creed . . . full legal

protection for these children is necessary . . . I fear irreparable harm unless immediate action is taken . . .

Following this letter the managers gave permission for Catholic children to withdraw from religious instruction. Prior to the 1902 Act the Catholic children would have had to have their scripture lessons in the Church of England school as there was no alternative Catholic school locally such as existed in the mainly urban boroughs. Under the new Act the Catholic priest was permitted to offer an alternative arrangement.

A teacher on obtaining a certificate should have been paid at a salary starting at £70 per annum according to the new regulations, and an uncertificated teacher would command a salary of £45 per year; however, there was evidence that in 1904 a certificated teacher at the Ambleside school was awarded only £60 p.a. Pupil teachers started at a salary of £25 per year, and monitors, girls under 18 who wanted to start pupilage, were given £8 per year.

Considerable tension existed between the School Managers and the County Council Authorities; there was constant friction over financial matters, about who paid for some maintenance costs, about capital costs, repairs and renewals, for instance provision of suitable desks and so on, but there was also friction about the role of the teacher. In spite of the new Act stipulating that from now on teachers were not to be considered as parish workers there is evidence that Ambleside was slow to change its ways. In 1906 a very strong letter was sent from Westmorland Education Department advising the Managers that

such a stipulation that a teacher will be required to play the organ in church or teach Sunday school is an imposition . . . the school may loose its recognition if it persists in making these demands.

Because there were two elementary schools in Ambleside, the Kelsick Boys' School, and the Girls' and Infants' School, two identical handwritten letters were sent from the education department about misuse of teachers time.

The local education department no doubt was attempting to define the role of the teacher, but there is evidence from the Ambleside oral history archive that teachers continued to be employed as unskilled labour.

I was the caretaker as well as the teacher . . . cleaner I should say. I rose at six to light this awful stove. I was paid 3/4d per month for the cleaning, and I had to provide the cleaning materials.

This lady interviewed was born in 1900, attended Ambleside Girls and Infants school, and revealed it was not only the teachers that were used for unskilled labour.

The three teachers lived in the school house and we went in groups and did the housework for them. We were taught from scratch you see, the proper way to clean windows, the proper way to clean brasses, the proper way to set the table. We were taught table linen darning . . . perfect hemming . . . we made pinafores . . . and the elaborate work that went into chemises. The vicar had seven sons and thats where we used to darn all their socks, at school . . . and it had to be done beautifully . . . the vicar in those days had staff.

It is of interest to note that Mr Hawkesworth had 'staff' at the vicarage, and although he complained at the small stipend when initially appointed, the assumption must be he had private means.

This respondent started teaching in 1908:

We started off of course with assembly, and after assembly we had religious instruction that was compulsory of course, and we had each week a bit of the old testament with the opening hymns and prayers, old testament one day, new testament the next, church history such as about the reformation and Thomas a Becket and people like them, and then psalm and hymn singing and another time repetition of texts of the bible and passages.

Arithmetic . . . tables were learnt by rote . . . it was a real sing-song, times table practice continually repeated aloud . . . they started long multiplication and long division when they were nine, and then went on to weights and measures, the compound rules, and in the upper classes they got to compound interest, money problems, stocks and shares . . .

If a child couldn't read fairly fluently by the age of eight he was given special attention. Reading aloud in turn was the regular practice, the children therefore could judge each other . . .

The scholars were all seated in long parallel desks which had four or six seats with backs upright, no fluttering hands or scraping feet, speaking only by permission and addressing the teacher as Sir or Madam. I didn't like Ma'am. Caning allowed if necessary, and girls too . . .

Pen and ink came in after 1910 . . . they had ink wells in their desks you see so they had to write in pen and ink and it was a bit messy, it was the ink, but they had to wipe up every drop of ink they spilled. I won't tell you what the handkerchieves were like.

A letter was sent to the Managers from the father of a girl who complained that a teacher had hit his daughter on the head with a stick: the complaint was dismissed, discipline had to be maintained. Another oral history respondent said

if the teacher says it is so it is so, we daren't answer back . . . children did not speak . . . you only spoke with permission.

After a considerable amount of discussion and persuasion the Kelsick Grammar School formally opened in Ambleside in 1908, giving 20% of the places free, and thus complying with the wishes of those submitting evidence to the Royal Commission in 1866: 350 pupils enrolled representing 'all classes' from Ambleside and District. The Headmaster, the Reverend J. Lewes was appointed out of 104 applicants. He had a first class Classic Tripos from Cambridge. Miss Smith was appointed to be in charge of girl boarders.

An oral history respondent said that Miss Roberts, the Headmistress of the Girls and Infants school at that time, was not happy with the idea that she would loose her brightest pupils to a grammar school at the age of 11, which meant she was left with what she referred to as the 'backward' ones.

Another girl remembers:

> When I was eleven I was in the top class, so for 12 and 13 I was marking time . . . I went to the vicar for french lessons, and in the last year they sent me down to the Infants school to sharpen pencils and help the teacher out which was not doing my education any good . . .

In fact the mother of this particular pupil was very keen for her daughter to go to the Grammar school and obtained extra coaching for her to go as a late entrant.

The daughter of the Headmaster of Langdale school remembered being in the school in about 1913.

> We wore pinafores, definitely pinafores. The boys all wore short trousers, they all seemed to be made of corduroy and as far as I can remember the boys always smelt rather badly. The girls had pinafores sometimes clean sometimes not, and longish frocks to about 8" from the floor and both sexes wore clogs, definitely clogs. You wore what we called low shoes on Sunday. The girls all had their hair in pigtails.
>
> We had needlework – I remember that very distinctly and my father taught scripture with great vigour . . . he never caned girls. Children brought sandwiches and there was a stove in the school that did the heating and they sat round the stove.

This respondent went on to Kelsick Grammar school

> we had a classical scholar from Cambridge as Headmaster and he looked at the local children in despair because no one had the slightest interest in latin or greek.

The children from the valleys who were fortunate to attend the Kelsick Grammar school had to board in Ambleside because there was no transport available, and this respondent did not go home for the whole of her first term. Most girls left the Grammar school at the age of 15.

Leisure

Leisure activities gradually increased; a reading room was opened at Rydal when a barn was converted for the purpose at a cost of £36; the local Squire Mr le Fleming of Rydal Hall gave £10 towards the costs. There were initially 53 people on the list at Rydal for the subscription library, and an appeal went out for pictures to go on the barn walls. Skelwith Bridge reading room continued to thrive, charging members 3d. per quarter.

Another library was started in Ambleside; the Robert Crewdson Library had 2,200 volumes and only required 2s. per year joining fee. This was a lending library and opened on Tuesday evenings between 7-8, Thursday afternoons between 2-3, and Sunday afternoons between 1.30 and 2.30. As well as a lending library it operated a News room which was open each weekday from 9 a.m. to 10 a.m. for men, but ladies could use it till 6 p.m. It had among the daily papers;- *The Standard, The Daily News, The Guardian, The Liverpool Mercury,* and *The Lancashire Post*. Among the weekly papers were: *The Westmorland Gazette, The Illustrated London News, The West Cumberland Times, The Carpenter and Builder, Work, The Temperance Chronicle,* and *The Christian Million*. The monthly papers were *Sunday at Home, British Workmen, The Leisure Hour,* and *The Band of Hope Review*.

In addition to library provision the church encouraged a parish concert to be held every fortnight, and lantern lectures were becoming very popular. By 1894 the popularity of both concert parties and lantern lectures was such there was often standing room only.

Leisure and sport continue to be mentioned in the Magazine; in May 1895 the Brathay Cricket Club match against Coniston had to be 'abandoned owing to the inability of Coniston to muster a team . . .'. However, by September of that year Brathay had acquired a houseboat and started a swimming club for youngsters and young men. The Council debated about creating a public swimming pool 'for lads to learn to swim'. There was concern following yet another drowning in the lake. The following year a Men's Club was started at Brathay and a programme of activities drawn up.

There was a perceptible change towards encouraging a variety of leisure activities, but not on Sundays. A letter was sent to the Furness Railway Company.

> *We, the Ambleside Urban District Council have observed with great regret that your Company has introduced a service of Sunday excursions to Ambleside. We feel it our duty to strongly deprecate such an innovation . . . it destroys the quiet of Sunday . . . it is most distasteful to the vast majority . . . it is highly prejudicial to the neighbourhood . . .*

The Council was at one with the vicar in deciding what was and what was not appropriate behaviour for Sundays.

However, over the first decade of the twentieth century there was a gradual sense of relaxation in what activities were permitted. The new King loved sport, and generally had a greater zest for life than his long widowed mother; and there was also a faint whiff of marital scandal. But perhaps the greatest thrill was the arrival of the motor car. In 1906 the Highways Protection League issued through the local Councils their recommendation that the

> *present limit for motor cars of 20 m.p.h. be reduced to 15 m.p.h., with lower limits in towns. Driving is an offence if it causes nuisance with noise, vibration, smoke and smell.*

Regarding head lights, it was recommended that the

> *maximum Candlepower be fixed. Licenses will be endorsed if a driver exceeds the speed limit twice.*

Transport offered to Stock Ghyll Falls.

Ambleside fixed a speed limit of 10 m.p.h. reducing to 5 m.p.h. round the Market Cross.

Whist drives became popular; permission was given for the Windermere Electricity Supply Co to lay a cable to the Assembly room; a piano was purchased for the infants school, and at the Mothers Union Christmas party in 1912 the magazine reported that blind mans bluff and musical chairs were played. Later in the year the Mothers Union were to take a motor coach for their annual summer outing. The vicar led the demand for a parish hall to be built where the young could gather for both religious and social purposes.

Tourism was increasingly important to Ambleside; and the Council realised they would have to advertise in local magazines to generated both wealth and employment. In 1909 the Co-operative Holidays Association responded to the advertisement and contacted the civic authorities to confirm they would like to take up 400 places in Ambleside between the months of August and July – but they would need bathing places. The Council took the idea up, and provided boats, life buoys and changing cubicles at Waterhead. When the lake bathing station opened the tickets cost 2/- per month.

Perhaps the most imaginative suggestion for increasing the number of tourists was the Council's announcement that:

Every facility should be granted to encourage the science of hydro aeroplaning in this District. This opinion is formed on a patriotic basis as the Council realises how backward England is, and the untold value to the whole vicinity that would be derived from such an advertisement as aeroplaning over Lake Windermere.

A speed limit of ten miles an hour was proposed for steam vessels on Windermere.

Health and Housing

Harriet Martineau wrote her famous letter of 1848 about some of the houses in Ambleside describing them as 'stinking holes', and Mary Armitt in her '*History of Ambleside*' written in 1906, described Rattleghyll as a 'mean and squalid quarter'. One common lodging house in Rattleghyll at this time had four attic rooms, two bedrooms, a common kitchen, a wash house and a w.c. and was 'suitable for twelve people'. Complaints were made to the Council about keeping unregistered lodging houses which now had to be inspected by the Medical Officer of Health. At one house the inspector recommended that

all windows had to be made to open, and ventilators fixed in attic rooms; the kitchen window to be made to open. The tramps lodging houses has to be disinfected.

In 1902 Bridge House, the little house built over the river, and later to become the icon of Ambleside, was inspected:

there are two apartments with total space of 408 cubic feet, and the Regulations stipulate there must be 300 cubic feet per adult. There is no water, privy or ash pit, but the occupier has the use of an ash pit, privy and tap from the yard behind. The arrangement from the sanitary point of view not good in terms of Public Health and housing of the Working Classes, but the Council cannot prohibit the house being tenanted, but can ask the proprietor to make provision . . .

In the years since Martineau's comments perhaps nothing much had changed by way of good working class housing provision, and it remained a topic on which the Church had little or nothing to say. Kathy Watson in her '*History of Ambleside*' writes of a review of local housing conditions undertaken by the Council in 1909 which illustrated the overcrowding that existed in many cottages, with many lacking provision of proper ventilation.

There were many cases with no water supply to the house . . . slops had to be carried to the gullies . . . pigs and domestic animals were kept in back yards . . . there was an open midden in the middle of Church Street . . .

The sewerage system put in place in 1895 was always inadequate for a population of around 2,000, but of course the numbers increased to 3,000 or more during the summer holiday season. There were frequent complaints about both the smells and the river pollution.

Under the new Housing and Town Planning Act of 1909 the Medical Officer of Health had powers to make closing orders on slum property if the situation could not be otherwise remedied, and following the housing survey the

Inspectors found about 115 houses to be substandard. There were voices raised in the Council about the feasibility of taking up new powers and 'take steps for the provision of Workmen's Dwellings'. This question was debated, but the Council was unhappy about financing any such initiative, and eventually a solution was agreed that private enterprise might be persuaded to build houses for rent. Nothing appears to have been done about the poor housing stock, and in 1914 the inspectors again visited the eleven houses in Rattleghyll. These houses had between them thirty bedrooms, and fifty inhabitants. The Inspectors commented that the 'roofs had to be raised to obtain better ventilation, windows had to be inserted, and the sanitary arrangements had to be improved' The Inspectors reported:

> that there were 113 houses that had both been inspected and needed improvement, a further 15 needed inspection, and there were by now 128 houses that were classified as being substandard.

In reply to a query from the Local Government Board as to how many houses were required to 'provide accommodation for persons of the Working Class' the Council resolved to reply that the answer was probably ten. The Council agreed that horses, cattle and swine may be kept in the back yards, but 'owners must comply with the bye-laws' regarding the removal of the midden.

As has been mentioned a Medical Officer of Health had been appointed under the Public Health Act of 1875 on a part-time basis. As well as overseeing

Road to the Falls.

the inspection of nuisances and insanitary housing, the main reason for state intervention in this field was because of the outbreaks of cholera, typhoid, and tuberculosis. In 1887 a suggestion came from Grasmere Local Board that the area should have its own Sanatorium, but there were no funds available. However, moves were made to acquire a site for an Infectious Diseases Hospital, and a plot near the Gas Works was investigated. There was also a suggestion that the Medical Officer of Health should become a full time appointment, but this would be feasible only if Ambleside combined with other Sanitary Authorities: the first doctor appointed was paid at the part-time rate of £12 per annum. Finally in 1893 the Council bought a wooden hut near Stock Ghyll park at a cost of £45, and, having spent £147 on the necessary alterations, the fever hospital duly opened in 1898. A hospital committee was created to oversee expenditure, and it was minuted that

> *three suitable bedsteads with spring and hair mattresses together with four chairs, two small tables, as well as a mangle and washing tub for use in the wash house*

be purchased. Later a 'suitable kitchen range' was bought. Information was given to the lodging house keepers about the dangers of small pox following an outbreak of four cases, and the Inspectors were given further instruction to disinfect the 'tramps lodging houses'.

When the hospital opened its doors to five cases of scarlet fever, a nurse was appointed. However, there was a problem over admission as there was

> *difficulty of getting a patient to the hospital at once as no one will lend their conveyance for such a purpose.*

The Committee debated about procuring an ambulance, but in the event shared one with Windermere. Hospitals at this time were not state run, they paid their way by charging patients, and by charitable fund raising, often organised by the churches. A municipal hospital had to decide whether to charge fees, and initially Ambleside Council agreed that parents of children with scarlet fever should not be charged. The hospital was run by a caretaker who was paid '2/6d a week regularly, and given three tons of coal, and given 10/- per patient per week'. The nurse cost 15/- a week, but a nurse was only hired when there were more than three patients. Less than that number were looked after by the caretakers wife. The purpose of the hospital was isolation.

In 1902 there was a conference in Kendal regarding opening a 'Westmorland Sanatorium for Consumption', and Ambleside agreed to send a delegation. There was also a suggestion from Dr Johnson, a local general practitioner, that the County Council should open a small pox hospital. At this time Ambleside cases of small pox were treated at Woodside Hospital, New Hutton, a considerable distance away, and questions were raised regarding both the charges of £5. 5s. per week, and the 'cost of the carriage of the patients'.

Although initially the Council had agreed not to charge the parents of children in the fever hospital, by 1905 this decision was reversed and a 'bill was handed to parents for cost of maintenance only during time of detention in hospital'. Many could not pay the charges, but 'their names were recorded' There was no doubt costs were mounting, and as it became apparent that patients clothing had to be disinfected, the committee had to consider investing in machinery. The Committee rejected a High Pressure Steam Disinfector at £160, and recommended purchase of the Thrushfield Low Pressure Steam Disinfector at £60. There was also the suggestion in 1905 that 'both the Council Offices and the hospital be put into telephonic communication'. However, the cost of 15 gns for connection by the telephone company was considered too much. Meanwhile the Clerk to the Council agreed to

write to all local doctors to obtain their terms for attending patients in the isolation hospital.

In the same year the Surveyor was asked to prepare plans for

small additions to the hospital in the shape of w.c's, a bathroom, and a lavatory, the latter to be supplied with hot water, all at expenditure of £65.

This was later amended to £40.

A Hospital Management Committee was to be set up to superintend management who drew up the following 'Rules of Admission'.

At least three hours notice was needed for patients to be admitted. No patient shall be admitted without a Certificate from the Medical Attendant stating the nature of the case. The Certificate shall be taken to the Inspector of the District whose duty it will be to procure the Ambulance. No patient to be discharged without permission from the Medical Officer of Health. Each patient shall bring a proper supply of linen for change and cleanliness but no more 'stuff' clothing shall be brought and the latter be left at the hospital on departure. No visitors or friends shall be allowed entrance unless sanctioned by the Medical Officer of Health. No spirits, wine or alcoholic drink allowed to any patient without sanction. Medical men shall procure the services of nurses and give notice on their departure. The Surveyor is to pay the nurses and arrange conveyance to the station. Patients will not be charged for their maintenance, but will pay for Medical Attendance, except in cases of poverty. Patients requiring one nurse will pay £3. 3s. per week, and if they need two nurses they will pay £6. 6s. Patients not requiring additional nursing will be charged only £1. 10s. per week, and a private room costs £3. 3s.

It was also agreed to draw up Matrons Rules. Initially the caretakers wife was expected to work in the hospital, and the appointment envisaged was self-evidently a joint one. The other curious fact is the matron appears to be both a servant to the nurses and their superior.

In addition to her duties as Caretaker the Matron shall when the hospital is occupied clean the nurses room, provide and cook food for nurses and patients, and wash clothes of both nurses and patients. She shall be paid 10/- per week when there are two or less patients, and 2/6 extra for beyond that number. The Matron has entire charge

Washday – early 20th century.

of the hospital, she is responsible for the furniture, the stores and supervision of the nurses. She shall suspend a Chart near each bed on which the Medical Officer of Health will enter the patients name, address, disease and treatment. She will note in a book the departure and arrival of patients. She will keep a journal or day book for accounts. She will disinfect the patients clothing, and disinfect the ambulance each time it is used.

In 1907, not surprisingly, the Matron/caretaker left; the hospital was unoccupied for four months, and then the Kelsick landlords gave the hospital notice to quit as they wanted the land for the intended grammar school. The Council tried to find other sites for a local fever hospital, but eventually all cases were transferred to Kendal.

Church Matters

The evangelical movement to spread the Christian message continued to gather momentum, and the vicar was pleased to observe that during Lent in 1906 he had a congregation of 400 for a weekday night. This figure has more significance than the traditional count on Easter Sunday because on that day the tourists would swell the numbers unrealistically. The numbers coming forward for confirmation increased year on year, and the Sunday school movement thrived. The Mothers' Union had been inaugurated; its aims were 'to uphold the sanctity of marriage', and a branch was duly started at St Mary's. This would, the vicar hoped, help consolidate the congregation and 'give women a role to play'.

A respondent from the oral history archive who was born in 1897 recorded the following in 1982.

My Dad left school at 8. He couldn't read. The church had a lot of people in, the farmers and all the workers I suppose, mostly working the land, they thought a lot of the church. Church was the centre of social life. It was the only place we had to go. You stayed in your surroundings you see. You couldn't miss church. It was one of those things, your Sunday duty.

Another respondent from Rydal, born in 1895 says much the same:

We used to put our Sunday clothes on and go to church, we were in the choir, we used to go home and change into our second clothes and then we'd do all sorts of jobs in the yards like the hens and such like, and then we'd change back again at night you see, never kept our good clothes on all day.

On a Monday morning, I can tell you, my four brothers and my father each had a Sunday suit and each had what they called a night suit that they went to the Reading room, that was eight suits and my fathers suit that he went boxing in that was nine suits. Every Monday morning I brushed those suits and folded them and put them away. There were four brothers shoes, and my fathers shoes, they were all to brush and polish . . .

. . . there was a woman a while back that wrote she was not going to clean her husbands shoes, that he should clean his own!

Equally pleasing to the vicar was the fact that the offertory money was at last increasing; this was no doubt due to the economic upturn. The church still had to raise considerable funds for the National school, and by 1910 had indeed raised the necessary £1,200 for the new infants school. The church also had to keep reminding the parishioners that the Ambleside beds in Kendal hospital had to be paid for.

The church income for 1908 was as follows:

Ecclesiastical Commissioners	£ 54 6s. 8d
North Staffordshire Railway	£ 39 12s. 0d.
Newcastle Gas Co	£ 55 0s. 0d.
Queen Anne Bounty	£ 36 0s. 0d.
Pew Rents	£ 33 12s. 0d.
Total	£218 10s. 8d.

Church expenses had to be covered by weekly donations from the congregation, but major expenditure had to be raised by appealing to the whole community.

In June 1910 the death of King Edward VIIth was announced, to be followed a year later by a June Coronation of King George Vth when the church organised a grand celebration. It began with the school children drilling, then sports for the children, a maypole dance, and finally a great bonfire was lit over Ambleside on Loughrigg. The Council announced that Coronation Day was to be a holiday, 'all shops should be decorated and show some signs of rejoicing'. A Loyal Address was sent from the inhabitants of Ambleside.

In January 1914 Hawkshead church magazine joined with Ambleside and Brathay and the cost of subscribing to the magazine went to 1s. per year. In August the Hawkshead parish magazine noted that the parishioners of Hawkshead 'may use the Ambleside Horse Ambulance van on payment of costs with an additional fee of 5s.'.

The Ambleside Council decided the time had come when they would have to 'inspect motor cars plying for hire within the District', and all pleasure boats had to be certified as safe. 'Touting for hire' remained a problem, with unlicensed carts and carriages. Permission was requested and granted from the Post Office Telegraph Department for telegraph lines to be laid in the Township.

The beginning of the welfare state

Sickness among the children remained a problem, which undoubtedly it was, and was constantly blamed for poor school attendance. One day in March 1911 only 11 pupils attended school at Skelwith from a roll of approaching 60. But perhaps if the church authorities had looked closely into the reasons for poor school attendance they might have realised that the children were working. This respondent was working from the age of ten for . . .

two hours before I went to school. I started at 6.30 . . . cleaning shoes and knives, filling coal boxes and riddling ashes and carrying out the ashes and I got 1s. 8d. a week. Then I'd a longer do on a Saturday 'cos I'd the yard to sweep and I'd to go in on Sundays as well, and then they raised it to 2/- a week. Then for two or three summers I took a gallon of milk to a house at the top of the hill every night and I got a penny for that.

I remember one year when I was cleaning shoes the frost was so bad it froze me blacking (shoe polish) . . . I'd only an outside shed to work in and there was no heat . . .

Medical costs continued to be prohibitive for the poor, but the first National Insurance Acts of 1911 gave some benefit to the wage earner. The intention behind the two National Insurance Acts of Parliament was to give limited financial aid to working people if they became ill, or if they became unemployed. The idea of the statute was that the employer, the employee, and the state would contribute equal thirds. This usually meant just the man of the house was covered for sickness costs, and for sickness benefit, and the women and children would receive no medical cover at all. Before 1911 if a man did not go to work he did not get paid. An employee of the Council once requested payment because he was ill, and was informed that the Council had no powers in this respect. The church was anxious to explain to local employers that in order for their employees to obtain full benefit from the new Act the employees had to join an Approved Friendly Society who would administer the scheme, and the Church Benefit Society was already active in the parish.

The Act also instituted an arrangement with the medical profession who took insured patients on to their 'panel' free, but this did not extend to the 'panel patients' family. The doctors bitterly resisted any thought of a state medical service, but they did get involved both with the 'panel', and with the new immunisation programme against diphtheria which was authorised by the Medical Officer of Health. The anti-toxin became available locally in 1910, and the 'Council was prepared to pay for all serum supplied by them to poor inhabitants'. In 1913 registration of tuberculosis became mandatory, and the question was raised whether cerebo-spinal fever and poliomyelitus should also be registered. The local smallpox hospital increased the number of beds to forty.

It should be added that in 1908 the Liberal Government did help the aged poor by passing the Old Age Pensions Act which ensured that a person over seventy with income below 10/- per week could be entitled to a pension of 5/- per week, and 7/6d if he was married. This was the first state benefit, and it was hoped that it might banish the fear the poorest had of ending their days in the workhouse.

Unemployment benefit also became available following an Act of Parliament in 1911 for some fully insured workmen, often paid through Trade Unions, but this benefit was only for a few selective industries and usually applied to the more skilled workers. Most unskilled labourers could not afford the contributions the insurance scheme demanded. If men became sick or lost their employment they still had to turn to the parish for relief.

The Trade Union movement, which had its origins in the craft guilds, had yet to spread its organisation to the ranks of the unskilled. Because of fear of unemployment the men largely worked the hours the employers asked of them, and the hours worked were very long. However, in the minutes of 1911 'it was recommended that the Councils workmen of the labouring class be allowed Saturday afternoon holiday'; this was in contrast to a decision to 'suspend the weekly half holiday in Ambleside from 15th May to 15th September inclusive for shop workers'. The tourist trade would require shops to be open for six days a week during the summer season.

Meanwhile the Medical Officer of Health closed Skelwith School down for two cases of Scarlet Fever, and Nurse Lee left Ambleside after 30 years service. A subscription leaving present of £200 was raised. The vicar wrote that

Ambleside patients cost Kendal Hospital about £170 per year, and local contributions towards this amount came to only a little over £10!

In 1911 a deputation of women rate payers petitioned the Council on the subject of urging the Government to grant facilities for the Parliamentary Franchise (Women's) Bill. The petition was signed by '15 male and 76 female rate payers'.

Their request was received grudgingly as minuted and came to nothing.

The First World War 1914-1918

In August 1914 Germany invaded Belgium and as a consequence Britain and France declared war on Germany. In September the vicar of Hawkshead, Canon Irving, wrote about this

terrible war which has come upon us so unexpectedly . . . and we have heard the stories of the barbarities of the Germans.

Moorman writes that

many clergy saw the war as a great crusade, a struggle between good and evil with the tacit assumption that all the good was on one side and all the evil on the other.

The Bishops became 'effective recruiting officers'. The debate the church conducted was whether the clergy should join up or not. The Archbishops thought it inappropriate for men of the cloth to fight, and in the event 'few clergy were combatants though many chaplains had positions of extreme danger'.

The men were volunteering quickly and within the first month of the war '10 men had come forward from Grasmere, and we should have 50 volunteers from Ambleside'. Hawkshead parish started a committee for relief work, and a rifle club for those over 16 years. Seventeen men from Brathay parish had enlisted by October 1914, some to the Lancashire Fusiliers, some to the Border Regiment, and others to the North Lancashire Regiment. The women from the parishes of Wray, Ambleside, Brathay and Langdale had made a total of 1,150 garments for soldiers and refugees by Christmas 1914. They also started a Christmas pudding fund for the men in France.

'England is not Perfidious Albion' wrote Canon Irving.

We must fight! The young men must obey the call to manly and heroic duty! Every able bodied man, certainly the unmarried of fitting age should follow the example of those who are nobly doing their best for their country.

Mrs Irving and her Bible class were helping to provide knitted cardigan jackets for the Indians who 'are in the fighting line but who are suffering from the cold'.

In November 1914 the Ambleside schools were inspected by His Majestys' Inspectors:

Ambleside was the worst offender in the district as regards child labour . . . Some children were working 30-40 hours a week outside school hours and were too exhausted to benefit from education . . . a reasonable amount of work is a good thing but . . . the Education Authorities will consult on legal action against parents and employers.

The evidence from an oral history respondent suggests that by 1917 nothing had changed.

When I was a lad of seven I was working, you know, as an errand boy and I got 1/- per week. My brother was a milk boy for 1/6 a week to all the houses up Skelghyll before school. I got another job later sorting potatoes . . . I was very frightened by the rats . . .

At Christmas the Ambleside church had 'its record number of communicants'. Many lads had got a few days furlough, and the vicar wrote that 'the healthy life, the exercise, the open air and the drill have done them untold good'. There were now 240 local young men in uniform.

In February 1915 Stanley Hawkesworth, the son of the vicar of Ambleside, was reported killed in action. His father wrote . . .

And further I say it, God knows in all humility if such a sorrow was to come to any home in the parish it should come first to the vicarage, where it ought to be borne with courage and resignation. If it were God's will that any young man were to lay down their lives for their Country, Stanley would be proud and glad to be the first.

Stanley Hawkesworth was going to become a Missionary.

Canon Irving wrote his message:

Pray without ceasing; knit socks without ceasing; let the faithful come to the Lords Table without ceasing; write to our soldiers cheerful letters without ceasing while they are doing their duty without ceasing.

Early in 1915 the Canon denounced those of military age who were 'lagging behind and smoking cigarettes'. Mr Heelis, husband of Beatrix Potter, was quoted in the Church magazine as saying 'that there were about 30 men who ought to go from the parish of Hawkshead'. In 1916 Canon Irving put a question in the magazine seeking out opinion.

Ought the names of those who are only now going into training, after slacking at home for 18 months or more be placed on the Roll of Honour in the church?

At Easter in 1915 in Ambleside there was an upbeat message from the vicar because there were 498 communicants; but by June 'everyone mourns'.

The Council put the annual rates up to 2s. 8d. A War Agriculture Committee for Westmorland was formed to advise on economy, and one of their first tasks was to consider the price of coal. A Recruiting Committee was also formed to advise men working on the farms about enlisting in the Reserve, but 'it would be up to the Local Tribunal to decide whether they were indispensable or not'. The farms became short of labour, and women were eventually recruited to work as agricultural labourers

In spite of the fact that the horrors of the war dominated the lives of the congregation, the vicar urged that the meetings of the Band of Hope and Temperance Society should still command every ones attention. However, meetings sometimes had to be postponed 'due to bereavement'. Canon Irving wrote:

This is a Holy War. Every man, woman and child should strive to bring this terrible conflict to an end.

The Brathay vicar shared this view:

. . . the call to work is imperative. The army is fighting, the wounded and the sick and the destitute need our help to the utmost.

In November 1915 the murder of Edith Cavell, a nursing sister working in a hospital in Belgium, shocked the country.

The ill-treatment of women and children is part of the Teutonic ethic of war . . . they have a cynical disregard of humanity . . . they are butchers . . . Men, ye that are men, enlist!

Enlist they did, and in January 1916 there were 270 men on active service from Ambleside and 50 men from Brathay. The vicar wrote about the district of Hodge Close where all the quarries were practically closed because the men were leaving. In spite of the high numbers in the armed forces, the vicar was able to report that so far 'only seven have given their lives for King and Country'. The vicar wrote that it was a

source of extreme joy and gratitude and pride to realise what a magnificent response Ambleside had made to the call for men.

There is no doubt that Ambleside did its duty nobly when it came to supporting the troops; the War Comforts Fund supported many and varied organisations, including the British Red Cross, the Prisoners of War Help Committee, the Equipment Committee at the Scottish Womens Hospital, the Wesleyan Army and Navy Board, Lady Monroes' Balkan Comfort Fund, the Serbian Relief Fund, the Number 16 General Hospital, the British Expeditionary Force, the Westmorland and Cumberland Yeomanry and the Mine Sweepers were some of the organisations aided by local charitable efforts. Brathay parish made just under 3,000 sandbags, the women made a 'huge number of garments,' and '3lbs of bullseyes were sent for the airmen'.

In April 1916 the Canon wrote:

Mrs Irving has wool and flannel especially prepared against lice . . . volunteers are wanted to make up shirts for the Suffolks . . .

Meanwhile the British Red Cross was raising funds for its hospital at Nutley, and it was intended various Counties would make a voluntary contribution. Funds were asked locally for money for an 'Ambleside bed in the Westmorland Hut' This Hut was to be built entirely by money subscribed by the County and would contain 20 beds. The Authorities were

wishful for the beds to be endowed . . . the upkeep of each bed is £65 p.a.

Ambleside Kinema Company generously devoted the proceeds of a special performance to the Ambleside Bed Fund and raised £108. 11s., and a further £11. 2s. was raised by donation. The contents of ten collecting boxes came to a further £4. 19s. 1d.; the whole amounted to funding for no less than three beds.

In July 1916 there was the horror of the battle of the Somme.

We are passing through a time of terrible crisis. Even those who never doubt the ultimate issue of this world wide war, all admit we may have to pay a big price for victory.

Brathay listed the work that was made and sent to the front: 118 Day shirts, 4 Helpless Case shirts, 17 Night shirts, 38 pyjamas, 46 vests, 12 Helpless Case Bed jackets, 14 Nightingales, 69 Bed jackets, 9 Enteric Night shirts, 22 doz Hankerchieves, 22 bandages, 14 pairs Bed Socks 328 prs Socks, 1 Body Belt, 12 Helmets, 7 Caps, 50 prs Operation Stockings, 2 prs Cuffs, 58 prs Mittens, 2 Scarves, 6 Towels, 6 Sheets, 9 Pillows, 3 Pillow cases, 3 Bolster cases, 6 Dusters and 18 Hot Water Bottle Covers. Brathay sent to the front in 1916 a total of 857 articles, and with 385 articles from Langdale, made a total of 1,242.

In the magazine there began to appear almost month after month the announcement that 'One more name is added to the Glorious Roll of Honour', and in 1916 a name of a soldier on active service in India was added. Canon Irving and the Master of the school have

given and prepared a Roll of Honour to hang in the school. Once a week while the war lasts, the boys will march past and salute.

The vicar of Ambleside felt he must write to urge teetotalism on the parishioners:

The man who systematically takes too much strong drink is the greater enemy to his country and the British Empire than the most unscrupulous German spy in our midst. The immoral man, he that does not show chivalry to womanhood, is on exactly the same level as those who were guilty of such monstrous offences in Belgium.

A letter on the evils of drink was delivered by the church to every house in Ambleside.

In the Hawkshead magazine in 1916, the following announcement was made.

2nd Lieut (Temp Capt) T. H. Irving was killed in action on August 19th while searching for his brother 2nd Lieut W. R Irving who was wounded the previous day while leading an attack on the German lines.

A priest from another parish wrote in the church magazine:

There are some things about this sad story which are very beautiful and touching – the wonderful affection of the two brothers – their comradeship in the field – their part in one of the most hard fought battles of this unexampled war – one brother wounded and the other going out to search for him at the imminent risk of his life, and himself struck down in the midst of his self-appointed task of desperate peril! He would have been proud to do his duty. Of all the noble lives which have been laid down in this war Tom Irving was amongst the brightest. The cost is heartrending and the end is not yet within sight.

In November 1916 seventeen year old James Hems was killed in battle. 'He would go' said his Mother. The vicar commented in the magazine

what a wealth of heroism there is in the words "he would go".

The vicar was able to express his conviction that this was a just war.

Some dear lad giving his brave life and some people talk at times of such being wasted lives; never was this a greater perversion of the truth . . . lives given for the cause of righteousness and justice are now living in a better world.

Throughout the war the church activities went on very much as usual, and Hawkshead was proud to announce that in 1916 the church had a Sunday School of six classes. The size of the congregations held up, and the ritual of the church year was maintained. Although the war and the consequences of the war dominated the church magazine, the vicar liked to remind the parishioners that the church had responsibilities to the schools. The Diocesan Inspector came to Brathay School and gave a very favourable report.

The Infants are being taught upon correct and modern lines . . . the upper division children know their Old Testament narrative, and repetition tasks were rendered excellently. The children showed a thorough knowledge of Christian Doctrine and the Catechism . . . the singing is melodious and reverent . . .

The Church offertory during the years 1916 and 1917 did not change, and the beneficiaries remained the Sunday School, the Day School, the Clergy Fund, the Waifs and Strays, the Home Missions, the Foreign Missions and Kendal Hospital. In 1917, it was reported,

Ambleside and its immediate neighbours benefited greatly by Kendal Hospital; there were 46 admissions over the past year with an average stay of 30 days. Thirty operations were performed, and the average cost per bed per week amounted to £1 10s. 0d. per week.

At the Annual meeting of the Ambleside Rural Deanery of the Church Defence and Instruction Society, an item came up on the agenda regarding divorce; they were asked to consider a proposed alteration in the marriage laws making three years separation a ground for divorce; they unanimously rejected the idea.

Gunner Giles Redmayne was awarded the Military Cross for conspicuous bravery in the trenches, the third military honour won by Brathay men.

At Christmas in Hawkshead the local War Committee sent 27 food parcels to the Front, and each parcel contained

plum cake, plum pudding, tin rations, 6 mince pies, 6 currant pastries, a quarter pound of tea, a tin of condensed milk, half a pound of mint toffees, two candles and a bar of soap.

The Brathay message at Christmas was as follows:

It is for us they are fighting, for us they are enduring wounds, and sickness and untold hardship. There are things waiting to be made. Every woman owes the men all the service she can render. Let us do more than we have ever done before.

Can you grow another potato? . . . rubbish must be cleared, bushes removed . . . walks reduced and weeds treated with less respect . . . the idea is to encourage women to handle the rake, the wheelbarrow and the spade.

The Government had announced that it would assist villages procure seed potatoes and other seeds at a reasonable price. Canon Irving wrote that

we must leave flowers alone . . . study thrift . . . do all we can to help our country, and we must remember that every single potato grown is something to the good.

Ambleside Council minuted that more potatoes and oats were needed, and they agreed to take over the land proposed for allotments. At this time the carters employed by the Council asked for an extra half penny per hour, and some councillors suggested they should all be sacked. The fire service was down to one fireman during the day, and the service was still 'called by messenger'. Firemen had proposed they be exempted from national service, having offered 'uniformity of protection from fire to both rich and poor,' but it appears they had to face the call up. Throughout the country waste paper depots were being set up for recycling purposes; the churches vigorously supported the action and appealed for all *obsolete books, almanacs, bills, invoices, time sheets, time tables, magazines and all paper except sand paper.*

In March 1917 there came a strong plea from the church in Ambleside.

Will readers of the Parish Magazine remember the Border prisoners of War and spare all they can to help them? The rations allowed them by the Germans are wholly inadequate. We must sent them food or they must starve. There are at present over 200 Border prisoners in the hands of the Germans, between 30 and 40 are the 11th Brigade Border men, and the Lonsdales. Any day the number of men may be largely increased. So far only two Ambleside men are reported prisoners in Germany. Collecting boxes will be found in several shops.

The Hon. Secretary of the local branch of the British Red Cross was Mrs Wordsworth of Rydal Mount.

There was concern expressed that food was becoming short, and the government urged restraint. The church pleaded that the congregations should –

ration themselves as a family in bread, meat and sugar . . . they should use 4 lbs of bread per week, or 3 lbs for those who made their own bread, meat 2 lbs, including bacon, ham, sausage, game, poultry and tinned meat, and less than one pound of sugar per family.

Later on in the year 1917 there was a Kings Proclamation on economy in the use of food which was read four times in the services at Church.

Careful use of all food is a duty which everyone must now practice otherwise he is helping the enemy.

In Hawkshead this theme was endorsed and it was reported;

Miss Samuel lectured for three hours to a goodly and interested company in the Gymnasium on the making of pulp fruit, and vegetable bottling and drying. It remains for us to Act and Save if possible the damsons and apples . . .

In 1917 Giles Redmayne was killed in action; he was the son of the benefactors of Brathay. He signed on at the very beginning of the war in a non-commissioned rank as a gunner.

Giles was universally loved not only by every officer, N.C.O. and men in his own battery, but also everyone in our Division including the General.

Whether because of the pain of bereavement from the death of his son, and the continuing losses suffered by his parishioners, Mr Hawkesworth felt he could no longer continue as vicar; the Reverend Bolland was appointed to take the incumbency.

In June 1917 the Government issued an appeal to 'all the Women of England' to go and work on the land. The thrust of the appeal was that food production had to be increased, and it was the duty of the women to come forward and work on the farms. The Church responded; 'Women of Westmorland will show their patriotism by volunteering to help farmers'. Women who volunteered would have to go before a Selection and Allocation Committee, and on being passed fit –

They would receive one free outfit which would consist of the following items: one pair of high boots, one pair of breeches, two overalls and one cap . . . Women would be trained free for three weeks when they would be taught to milk cows, feed stock, and clean out shippons and pig styes. The pay would be 18/- per week, or 6/- for those who lived in.

Not only were women being urged to work on the farms, the Government indicated that 'experienced women' were wanted in France to work behind the lines to relieve men who would then become available to go to the trenches. The women were to go out and work as clerks, cooks, laundresses and 'all classes of domestic workers'. They would be working well behind the firing line,

but only women over the age of twenty and under the age of 60 need apply, and there were no facilities for training.

In 1917 the United States entered the war, and as a 'compliment to our latest ally the Star Spangled Banner was sung' in Ambleside church. The vicar wrote that the

Roll of Honour for the Noble Army of Martrys is showing the share that Ambleside is taking in the terrible price paid for the freedom of the world.

By November 1917, 34 men from Ambleside had died, but the numbers would increase.

In Hawkshead Canon Irving continued to press for people to save on food, and he published what he thought would be an appropriate specimen for a days rations:

For breakfast 2 oz bread, porridge using 1 oz oatmeal per person with 2 oz milk, 2 oz bacon, minimal sugar, minimal margarine and tea. For dinner 3 oz of meat per person, with 2 oz rice or beans or lentils followed by a 5 oz milk pudding with stewed apples. For tea there would be 3 oz bread, 2 oz cheese, sugar and cocoa. Cheese and beans give as good a body building result as meat. Maize is said to be as nourishing as wheat.

In November the Chairman of the Rural Food Committee was quoted in the magazine that he had . . .

now ascertained that the harvests of the world would not meet the requirements of ourselves and our Allies during the next twelve months unless the present rate of consumption is materially reduced.

The Reverend William Heyes from Langdale was anxious to get as near as he could to the front line in France. He had problems getting a passport, but in July 1917, after a lot of persistence he finally obtained one, and was able to set up a Church Army Hut which sold tea, biscuits, cigarettes and chocolate to the men from the trenches. The enterprise was not to make money, but just to break even.

Canon Irving appealed for a photograph of every man on the Roll of Honour; he wanted to put the photographs in an album which would be lodged in a safe place, as this 'would be of interest and value in the years to come'.

A letter was quoted in the magazine from 'one of our fighting boys' who wrote to his mother.

I was glad of the fags. I had just come out of a big fight, one of the biggest I have every been in. We gave the Germans H... They would not fight but threw up their arms and cried for mercy. I was two days and nights cut off from my battalion and without food. I have no news to tell you so I will close.

Canon Irving felt it his duty to keep reminding his parishioners of the fact that this was a just war, a war that had to be won whatever the cost. He wrote the following in May 1918:

By the pictures of the murder of Nurse Cavell, and the sinking of the Lusitania, the atrocities in Belgium and Serbias agony, and such like flagrant instances of Germanys attempt to terrorise we realise the kind of unscrupulous Hun our men are fighting. We are fighting that peace, mercy and liberty may be the birthright of our race.

Meanwhile in Ambleside the

dread results of the war have been falling heavily on our men in the last two months, four more are dead, and another seven missing.

The village women continued to make garments, and the Diocesan Inspector, although pleased with the pupils religious knowledge, was very satisfied to see the girls in Skelwith school had contributed to the war effort by making

150 pairs of socks, 18 pairs of mittens, 12 sleeping caps 2 helmets, 8 pairs of operational stockings, 3 pairs of gloves and 11 scarves.

A great plea went out for the people to go out into the woods and collect sphagnum moss, 'either wet or dry but it must be free of grass'. The magazine went on to state that the moss should then to be taken to a Miss Coffee in Ambleside, and she would forward it to France to be used as surgical dressing. A Matron at a clearing station in France was quoted as saying 'It is more precious than gold'; it was most important because of its antiseptic properties.

Hawkshead gave Lady Harrowby space to advertise her scheme for the 'entertainment of overseas convalescent officers who will stay in the Lake District in pairs for a fortnight'.

In Ambleside it was noted that

three of the older inmates in St Anne's Home have just left and gone into service. Four new children have just been admitted.

The Home was doing what it was intended it should do, which was to train the girls to become servants.

The Council meanwhile was concerned to maintain both the afternoon and Sunday post. Their other concern was whether

to continue to advertise that the District was being provided with the necessary food for visitors.

In August 1918, so wrote the vicar of Brathay,

Mr Hoover, the American Food Controller has assured us that the acute peril of famine is past as America is able to send us food. Meanwhile the war work must go on, garments must be made and the supply of eggs for the wounded in hospital must continue . . . The Government want 30,000 Female Recruits for the Army to work as clerks, cooks, waitresses and domestics.

Hawkshead recorded on the death of Tom Armer

he left you the greatest message of all, a life silently laid down for those he loved . . . he was counted worthy to be one to give his life for so great a cause.

Although towards the end of 1918 the news from the front gradually appeared to be more cheerful, the magazine emphasised how important it was to economise on coal, and why it was the duty of everyone to save it. There was also a message that 'nut shells and plum stones were required for munitions, but they should be thoroughly dried first'.

In Ambleside November 1918 the vicar wrote:

The influenza scourge is raging through the country and is being felt very heavily in the parish where there have been two deaths so far. The three Ambleside schools are closed because of the epidemic. Mrs Walker had just lost her second son, the first killed in action, the second died of influenza.

At the Armistice the vicar wrote . . .

it is with thankful hearts we record the fact that the church service on November 14th was very full.

In Hawkshead Canon Irving included the following in his address: A friend writes:

I suppose all you ----- pacifists will be clamouring for peace with dear Germany urging let bygones be bygones . . . Keep 'em in hell – on Christian teaching till in penitent sackcloth they have paid up . . .

Sixty-seven men from Ambleside were killed in the war; sixteen from Brathay and twenty-one from Hawkshead.

CHAPTER THREE

'Reader Pause and Think!'

The death toll from the Great War was simply colossal: almost 750,000 men from the United Kingdom and almost 250,000 men from the Empire and Dominions were killed in battle. Added to this number another one and a half million men were permanently damaged from wounds or from the effects of gas. Almost twice as many Frenchmen as British were killed. Civilians suffered many hardships but few casualties.

The men came home from the war to promises made in the General Election of 1919 that they would 'live in a land fit for heros'; the promises were for work and decent housing. They came home to a country burdened by the huge debt caused by the war which, according to A. J. P. Taylor in his book *'English History 1914-1945'*, amounted to over £9,000 million. World markets were in chaos, and the election promises came to nothing. Following mass demobilisation unemployment rose and by 1921 was over the 2,000,000 mark. Unemployment fell again towards the end of the decade, rose again in the early years of the 1930s to around 3,000,000, and never fell below 1,000,000 until the outbreak of the second world war.

Not only was there no work, but there was a huge shortage of decent houses for rent nationwide, and the big cities had a vast amount of slums to clear. One of the great reforms that took place during the war was the creation of a Ministry of Health which took over many of the responsibilities previously carried out by the Local Government Boards. Following the 1919 general election the new Minister for Health ordered the Local Authorities to build houses and let them at controlled rents which would be met by a Government subsidy. What this move did was to establish for the first time the concept that housing was part of a social service, but this nostrum would have little impact on the Councillors of Ambleside.

Women were given the vote in the general election of 1919, but only for those over the age of thirty. It was not until 1928 that women achieved parity with men and were able to vote at the age of twenty-one; however, even if women were given the vote they were far from emancipation: equality in other spheres was a long way off. Another reform carried through was the decision to maintain the restriction imposed in 1914 on the hours public houses were allowed to open. The church had been campaigning for forty years or more for a cut in the opening hours of public house, and they rejoiced at any curbs placed on the consumption of alcohol.

The Church magazine

Apart from writing about the need to fund the Christian Mission, and the perennial problem of funding education, two themes dominate the church magazine for the twenty years from 1919 to 1939. The first theme was the quest for peace, and the second the dire consequences of unemployment. During this period of time there was considerable evidence that not only Disraeli's two nations still co-existed, but how little attitudes had changed towards the problem.

The vicar of Ambleside reported that the Chancellor of the Exchequer was desperately wanting people to purchase War Saving Certificates to fund the cost of the war. The Chancellor was asking for no less than £25,000,000 to be raised nationally every week, and the vicar urged the congregation to buy as many saving certificates as they could afford.

The Archbishop of Canterbury appealed for funds to recruit to the Ministry: there were more than 2,000 candidates from the forces willing to train

and they must reach high educational standards . . . there is also a need for better payment and better pensions . . .

The Archbishop wanted to raise £5,000,000 to cover the costs, and part of the money raised should go to the schools which 'should all have genuine religious instruction' . . . Appeals for money to help the existing clergy followed because the aim of the Church was 'to obtain sufficient funds to pay all Incumbents £400 per annum'.

At the conference of Bishops some voiced the hope that the

barriers of caste and class will be widely broken down after the war. Practical religion will always be valued but there is a need for short bright intelligible services to be held everywhere.

Although on the surface the Church of England appeared healthy enough, the Bishop of Carlisle, in October 1923 noted that in his Diocese there were 50 incumbents who received a stipend of less than £250 per year, and 56 more who received less than £300. 'No one can keep up a vicarage, bring up a family and do work without anxiety on that income'. The vicar would still expect to be able to employ some domestic help, and no doubt he would still hope to be able to educate his children at a private school.

Throughout the two inter-war decades the church tried to get its finances into sufficiently good shape to be able to offer a decent living to the new recruits. In 1924 the Bishop of Carlisle gave a fête at Rose Castle in

aid of the Laymans Fund for the Augmentation of Poor Livings in the Diocese . . . clergy must have at least the bare necessities of life and the laity are generally opposed to the amalgamation of small parishes.

61

In 1925 the House of Bishops met to consider the Revised Prayer Book (Permissive Use) Measure of 1923. Work on the revision had been going on since 1908.

In an age which has witnessed an extraordinary revival of spiritual life and activity the Church has to work under regulations fitted for a different condition, and Elizabethan ideas of administration are no longer applicable.

The revised prayer book, which came into use in 1927, altered the marriage service and gave women the option to choose whether or not to vow to obey their wedded husbands.

Throughout these post-war years there was a constant plea often voiced by the Church Missionary Society for 'world evangelism as never before'. Missionaries came to Windermere and 'preached about the World Call' in a manner that can only be described as 'inspiring'. In 1921 an enormous effort had been put into the various Missionary endeavours which included giving support to – 'The Society for the Propagation of the Gospels' for (i) our own Countrymen abroad and (ii) the 'heathen'. Then there was the 'Church Missionary Society', the 'Zenana and Melanese Missions', and nearer home for the Mission in East London; and again the Church continued to work among refugees in France, Austria, Poland and Russia'.

The starvation in Russia 'the horrors of which are indescribable' demanded a separate appeal. Hawkshead appealed for money for

the starving children of Central Europe . . . the smallest sum or a single piece of soap or even a rag will be acceptable and it may be earmarked for a particular country.

The church was proud to announce that

A Picture Film by the Church Missionary Society will be shown on the Mass Movement in India depicting the village potter, oxen treading out corn and instructing outcasts etc.

Another film of the 'Burial of the Unknown Warrior' in Westminster Abbey was also shown. Locally the congregations remained large, and the numbers coming forward for confirmation most satisfactory. The Sunday School at Hawkshead was increasing, and held classes in both morning and afternoon. Ambleside started a scheme to deliver envelopes to every household to aid giving, 'even if it is only 1d. per week we must pay our debt, we must give alms, and we must spread the Faith'.

Meanwhile the choirmen were returning from France, and the vicar was pleased to note that in 1919 he had no less than 466 communicants at Easter. This is a high number and it is unlikely at that time the number would be greatly swollen by many visitors.

The church was getting into its pre-war confident swing again. Congregations were getting 'larger and livelier'; bible study for those over seventeen was started, and a separate class began for those in the 14-17 age group. Boys and girls had separate classes at Sunday school. In January 1921 the vicar commented that although there were between 40 and 50 attending Bible study classes but . . .

there are still many children who apparently go nowhere on a Sunday and this is not what it should be . . .

Later in the year he wrote:

Irregularity at attending Sunday School was bad . . . an irregular child was apt to grow into an unreliable adult . . .

The church revived the Band of Hope meetings; before the war Brathay Men's Club had 24 members of the Band of Hope, but 'five had died for their Country and of the rest only ten returned to Brathay'. On this point the vicar of Ambleside wrote that 'many men have still not returned and there may not be work for them to do here' . . .

Apart from raising funds for overseas missions the local charities were in need of financial support. The Ambleside Waifs and Strays Society 'in these difficult times is in debt'. Over the year it was noted that Ambleside had raised no less than £121 17s. 8d. for Kendal Hospital. Money was also needed at home for more mundane matters; for instance installation of electric light in St Mary's Church: the church at Hawkshead were also appealing for money to 'buy some sort of power to both blow the organ and light the church'.

The number of those coming forward for confirmation – Ambleside had 104 in 1920 – continued to give satisfaction, and the social branch of the church also continued to flourish. The Hawkshead choir grew to twenty seven. Brathay parish meeting discussed the formation of a Women's Institute; W.I. meetings were to be of an educational and social nature, and the aim was to help try to raise both awareness of the problems faced by women in rural areas, and to promote practical ideas to improve the standard of living. (In fact it was noted later that no great interest was shown by village women in the idea of forming a Women's Institute which was probably considered too middle class.)

In Hawkshead it was agreed that the proceeds from the Hawkshead Operatic Society was to be divided between the 'Soldiers Arrival Fund' and 'anything that can be got up to celebrate the home coming of those that have survived the war.' Writing in the Parish Magazine in July 1919 the Canon wrote

for the Hawkeshead Peace Celebration it was agreed that there should be a church service, sports pageant, tea for children and old people, a meat tea for the men who had served in the war, and dancing to be included in the programme.

In Ambleside a Thanksgiving Service was held in July 1919; it was 'excellently attended' and the vicar was able to 'welcome back the Choir-master from Salonica'. Ambleside held a Peace Celebration Saturday, *with a peel of church bells, childrens sports, adult sports with fell racing, teas, a Parade through Ambleside with the Town Band, and at 11 p.m. the mountains were lit up with flares, bonfires and fireworks.*

A war memorial to the fallen, designed by Austin and Paley, was commissioned.

Arrangements were made to unveil the Hawkshead War Memorial on the 11th. November 1920 to the twenty-one men who died: the Ambleside War Memorial to the 68 men who died was not yet ready. The church had a service on the 11th of November at 8 a.m., and at 11 a.m. with two minutes silence, and again at 8 p.m. when there was a Choral Thanksgiving and Memorial Service.

Four months later in March 1921 the Memorial to the Ambleside fallen was ready with the 68 names inscribed on Kirkstone slate;

theirs was a noble life . . . greater love has no man than he lays down his life for his friends . . .

The laying up of the Colours and the Dedication of the Memorial to the fallen in Kendal Parish Church was conducted by the Bishop of Carlisle: 'ex-service men, especially from the Border Regiment were cordially invited to be present'. The Brathay War Memorial Dedication for the thirteen from the parish who gave their lives took place in September 1921; the Last Post and Reveille were sounded by a bugler from the Lancashire Fusiliers.

In November 1922 Earl Haigs fund for disabled soldiers began selling the Flanders poppy.

On 11th November 1923 the vicar of Hawkshead said:

We are the Dead, they say, a short time ago we lived, felt dawn, saw sunset glow, loved and were loved and now we lie –

Education nationally

Although the general public seemed to remain indifferent to the state of the public elementary schools, the war did stimulate some new ideas on education. The Fisher Education Act 1918 raised the school leaving age from 12 to 14 and there was debate on the provision of secondary education for all. Marjorie Cruikshank writes that the old problems continued as before, and essentially the difficulty remained that the churches could not meet existing commitments, never mind contemplating raising the monies to build the necessary secondary and technical schools. But even though the churches could not afford the current costs, under no circumstances did they want their role to be taken over by the state. Fisher had wanted to take all 'non-provided' schools into the Local Authorities control in return for increased provision of facilities for denominational instruction. Cruikshank points out that some of the Anglicans had 'moved on' from their fierce opposition in 1902, and indeed some church schools became state schools, but many remained in violent disagreement. There was a rift in the previously united ranks of the church. In the event the Fisher Act did not amount to much; there was a shortage of money, so much needed rebuilding after the war, and education continued to have a low priority.

Although the Fisher Act raised the school leaving age to 14, the proposal to institute part-time education up to the age of 16 was not implemented. In 1922 Sir Eric Geddes presided over a Government expenditure committee and recommended sweeping cuts. What became known later as the 'Geddes axe' fell particularly harshly on education; school budgets were slashed and teachers had their salaries cut. However, on the good side, teachers salaries became uniform throughout Britain for the first time, all Education Departments had to offer the same salary rates, and the teaching profession became eligible for pensions. After the 'Geddes axe' the free places offered by local authorities to grammar schools became more limited.

If the old sectarian arguments on religious teaching were dying down, the controversy regarding overall costs of education remained active. Financing education was the largest issue local authorities had to deal with, and there is little doubt many authorities offered a poor education to the children. In 1926 the Hyde report suggested raising the school leaving age to 15, and the report also proposed a system of secondary education for all children. There were major economic difficulties at this juncture, and combined with general lack of interest these proposals were postponed until after the end of the second world war.

Education locally

Canon Irving was constantly berating the fact that Hawkshead had no Grammar school. The ancient Grammar school, attended by William Wordsworth, was closed down in 1909.

> We have lost the key . . . there were in 1919 17 applicants for three scholarships in Ulverston . . . the rest will suffer . . .

The Ambleside Parish Magazine announced with great pride the news that two pupils from Skelwith School had won scholarships to Ulverston Grammar School; the magazine did not say if the pupils were able to avail themselves of the scholarship; the distance was too far for daily travel.

The Skelwith School Report by the Government Inspectors on 23. 7. 1920

> reflects great credit upon the Master and his Assistant. The children show pleasing interest both in books and their beautiful natural environment . . . their speech, singing and drawing reveal careful and effective training.
>
> The Master has converted an old school desk into a joiners bench with tools given him by friends, and boys have made useful articles to develop handiness: it would be good for girls to have corresponding opportunities in domestic subjects.

The church schools continued to be inspected by two organisations, and three months later in October, the Skelwith School was duly inspected by the Diosecan Inspector. He was equally well pleased with the progress made by the pupils. He found

The prayer book portion of the syllabus had been carefully prepared . . . well chosen pictures of scriptural subjects give help to school work.

The vicar of Hawkshead wanted to make Hawkshead a

centre for advanced and practical instruction which would include . . . Rural Science, Practical Mathematics, Rural Carpentry, and Domestic Subjects.

The vicar wrote that he wanted a separate school for those over the age of eleven, and 'maybe children coming from over two miles would get a cycle allowance'. Even if this idea did not receive support for the necessary funding, evening classes for adults in cookery and joinery were started.

The Head Mistress of the Girls' National School since 1899 resigned and . . .

the Diocesan Inspectors would like to record their appreciation of her services in the great cause of Religious Instruction in the young. She was a powerful influence for good in the after lives of girls . . .

The school did not wait long for a replacement; a Miss Winifred Cloudsdale had passed her Northern Matriculation exams and was thus qualified to take over the Headship of the school. She was described as a most devoted Sunday Scholar and a member of the choir. Unfortunately she was not in post for long because her mother died, and the school managers agreed that it was her duty to give up her career to look after her father.

A respondent quoted from the oral history archive became a pupil teacher just after the end of the war. She was paid 6d. a week as a pupil teacher and 19/6d at the end of her pupil teachership in 1920. By 1945 her earnings had increased to £4 a week. In the interview she was asked about poverty among the Ambleside children, and her reply was,

there were no ragged children there . . . that was because Ambleside had become known as a tourist resort and their mothers were quite conscious about their childrens appearances and the houses were beautifully clean . . .

There were two ways of becoming a teacher; a recruit could either go to college from a grammar school, where it would be expected they would study and qualify in English, Maths, Geography, History, French, Latin, and Religious Knowledge, or they could become qualified by becoming a pupil teacher. The same respondent who qualified in 1920 said

teaching geography was teaching the Empire, not much else, then Scott of the Antarctic and the loss of the Titanic.

This lady became a supply teacher, and recalled that for weeks on a Sunday afternoon she walked ten miles over to Patterdale, and then walked home after school on a Friday afternoon. She also recalled that

I had to get up at six to light the stove and re-lay it and get it going. The children walked between 3 and 5 miles to school even in thick snow . . . we had the old tortoise stoves and we used to keep a kettle and a pan of water and have a hot drink at dinner time . . . the children brought sandwiches and we made them cocoa.

Discipline remained as harsh as it had always been, as recalled by this respondent –

if you weren't at school by 9 o'clock, well you got the cane, one stroke across each hand you know.

Ambleside Urban District Council

The reports on the condition of housing in Ambleside before the war indicated that many were substandard. There is evidence that the 'stinking holes' described by Harriet Martineau in 1848 were still lived in, and there remained many cottages that were unsatisfactory in respect of both overcrowding and sanitation. A respondent from the oral history archive described Bridge Street, the notorious renamed Rattleghyll, as follows . . .

families in there, the houses were two up two down, they all had big families and some had eight or ten kiddies living in there and you know there weren't bunk beds in those days, they were sleeping head to toe you know, or else on the floor. They were hard times.

I don't know if you have ever seen them, Carr's flour bags, the white ones . . . well all working people in those days got them from the grocer. When the flour bag was empty, wash them and they make good pillow cases. We hadn't a towel . . . I bathed many a time in a bucket. There was a terrible amount of poverty; all the working people had a hard bringing up . . . they lived on lights and sheeps hearts . . .

The new Ministry of Health, which had taken on overall responsibility for housing, wrote a letter to the Council in 1919 asking what active steps Ambleside intended to take to remedy the situation. A letter was sent back to the effect that as there was no overcrowding, no housing scheme was contemplated. The Housing Commissioner replied that the Council was 'under statutory obligation to formulate a suitable scheme . . .'.

Years later in 1930 a report was sent to the Council from the County Medical Officer of Health.

Houses are urgently required and there are houses that should be condemned as unfit to live in. It is high time that records should be made of all houses in your district in accordance with the Housing Consolidation Regulations of 1925. Had this been done I have no doubt the Council would have seen the necessity of expediting the provision of suitable accommodation for the inhabitants of this district. I would urge the Council most strongly to carry out a building scheme as soon as possible.

Rattleghyll – early 20th century.

The council eventually drew up a scheme for 34 'parlour and non-parlour type houses, all to be fitted with gas cookers and back boilers in the living room'. This scheme was later to be modified to a scheme for eight houses of the 'non-parlour type'. In 1932 the Council received another circular about the slum clearance scheme, and in due course of time notice was served on the landlords that the houses they rented out in Bridge Street were 'not fit for human habitation'. Houses in other parts of the township were also condemned.

The problem for the Council was they remained divided on the issue about whether it was their duty to provide houses. The Council also pondered if it should provide the unemployed with meaningful work, and should the unemployed be made to work for their benefits? The Womens Citizens Association sent the Council a petition urging speedy action on housing provision, but by the time the Council was dissolved on 31st March 1935 the houses had still not been completed.

The Council came into being initially to act as a sanitary body, to enable every house to have a supply of clean water, and a decent system of sanitation. The sewage system put in place at the end of the nineteenth century was never adequate, and the Council was, as ever, reluctant to spend ratepayers money. There is little doubt that the sanitary arrangements of licensed premises as well as domestic housing were both unsatisfactory and inadequate. In 1930 the Council minuted

> *It was resolved that the owners of the Royal Oak, the Waterhead Hotel and the White Lion Hotel be requested to provide proper urinal and water closet accommodation for the use of customers.*

Likewise it was minuted

> *The attention of H.M. Inspectors be drawn to the absence of lavatory accommodation at the bottling stores in St Mary's lane.*

The Council was aware of problems caused by the unlicensed slaughter houses, but even after slaughter houses had to be inspected under the Act of 1933, fears about cruelty to animals continued to be expressed by the R.S.P.C.A.

One of the problems caused by the slaughter houses was the disposal of the refuse which in all probability was left to rot. In 1927 the rate payers brought an official objection to the

> *smells caused by butchers offal and fishmonger refuse which must in future be removed and deposited at the sewage works.*

An oral history respondent recorded

> *there were loads of rats in those days, there were no dustbins – you'd go down these back streets and there wasn't a dustbin . . . Council would empty the ashpits periodically . . . there were these earth lavatories . . . if you got a rat's tail and took it to the Council you'd get 3d. for it.*

The Council sent out a circular requesting householders to burn as much refuse as they could on the kitchen fire, and they also made a plea for people not to throw tin cans and broken crockery in the river. A further concern to the Council was the discharge of bilge and oil by the boats into the lake.

The other concerns of the Council remained unchanged; planning applications had to be vetted, on street parking caused mounting concerns, and consideration had to be given to the question of

> *providing suitable stands for private motor cars belonging to persons requiring to stay only for a short time for the purpose of shopping. A Police Sergeant will direct private cars.*

Because of the annual increase in the amount of traffic it was minuted in 1928

> *we must have a bi-pass as soon as possible in order to relieve the excessive amount of heavy and other traffic.*

Touting for customers by men working for the hotels could be construed as a 'nuisance' if allowed to go unchecked. The Council decided that

> *as there was no industry of any importance carried on in the district therefore no increase in supply of electricity is anticipated.*

If the Council showed lack of concern in the housing problem, they was angry about the National Political League. The following item was minuted in 1922.

This Council deplored the existence and rapid growth of Proletarian Sunday schools which by their teaching of sedition and Revolution and their Blasphemous treatment of all Religion are fast becoming a menace to the stability of the democratic Constitution of this country as well as to our National Character, moral standards and home life.

There was no evidence that this movement made any headway with the people of Ambleside.

Church Street – early 20th century.

Health

The question was raised in February 1919 by Canon Irving in Hawkeshead 'Ought we to have a District Nurse?' This question could have been triggered by the influenza epidemic that swept the land. The Council was concerned, and suggested a voluntary aid detachment 'such as was in vogue during the war be used as Home Helps'. They decided to issue 1,000 leaflets on 'flu prevention'. The question about having a nurse was about money: the argument was whether the population should be provident and pay personally for the service, or whether the costs should be borne by an increase in either local or central taxation. Or alternatively 'should we just go on as we are?' The matter led to a deep discussion on the desirability of having a nurse who would also look after the villages of Sawrey, Wray and Graythwaite. The cry went out – 'there must be a public meeting!' The parish finally resolved the difficulty of finding sufficient funding for a district nurse, and appointed a Miss Filkin. 'It will be necessary to raise £160 a year for her salary'. An endowment fund had been started, and by 1920, had already raised £500, and 'it would be expected that anyone wanting the nurse would pay a minimum of 2/6 into the fund'. Without a wage and without benefits, money would be hard to find for many people.

By March 1924 the church had a deficit of £20 towards the nurses salary. A month later the nurse was appealing for 'bundles of linen rags' to use as dressings. By the end of that year the parish was holding 'sales' to raise money because the nurse 'needed a car'. At the same time Ambleside held a house to house collection for the Hospital in Kendal.

A circular letter to Ambleside Council from the Ministry of Health was received in 1926 inviting a discussion on women's health

with reference to Medical Services at Maternity Centres being available to persons desirous of advice on contraceptives.

The Council decided to ignore the circular. Sickness benefit was far from universal and did not cover the medical needs of the family. In order to afford medical care, and if financially prudent, families took out their own insurance policies with the Friendly Societies, and this insurance could cover the cost of doctors bills, hospital costs and funeral expenses. The Sons of Temperance, the Oddfellows and Hearts of Oak were some of the Friendly Societies that flourished locally.

The Church Magazine

Perhaps the relationship between church and Urban District Council had always been strained because in some way the Council had usurped the role the church used to occupy. In any event the vicar of Ambleside, Mr Bolland wrote an angry letter in September 1921.

The rates on the vicarage this half year amount to £18. 13s. 1d. The vicar as a loyal and patriotic citizen has delighted hitherto in paying his rates but when he sees the Parish inundated with unnecessary officials such as a lady inquirer for defectives, cigarette smoking inspectors of workrooms, and an off-come nurse, a school attendance officer, a man employed to see that children are not employed under the age of twelve, and we are now to have our own special 'sanitary' official, and the like he does begin to jib. There is not one of these things that cannot be done and more efficiently by Clergy or Sergeant of Police or District Nurse and at no extra cost to the community.

It would seem highly unlikely that the church would really want to take over from the elected representatives and their paid staff, or indeed be capable of such a move, but it does reflect an interesting increase in Council employees.

The Parish Church Council had recently started with ten elected members and six ex-officio members. The magazine noted that –

It had been proposed there should be five men and five women elected, but this was altered to seven men and three women,

but the magazine failed to elaborate on how it perceived future development. The Parochial Church Council (Powers) Act was passed in 1921, and the Bishop of Carlisle writing in the Diocesan Gazette says

Church Councils have a legal status with definite duties and are part of the constitution . . . their most important function is to co-operate with the Incumbent in the spiritual work of the parish . . . not so much in the efficiency of church business but in the sobriety and chastity of the parish they represent . . .

The Bishop noted the importance of keeping up foreign missions, and wrote:

one power conferred by the recent Act is the power to make and collect a voluntary Church rate which may prove in the future to be of the very highest importance.

Mr Gladstone had abolished the church rate in 1868, and although the Bishop of Carlisle expressly stated a return to a church rate would be voluntary if reintroduced, nevertheless it would be highly controversial and probably non-productive. In the event nothing came of the suggestion.

Later in the year the magazine noted there was an increase in the number of unemployed men. There had also been a failure of the harvest. Only the Band of Hope remained 'full of joy and pleasure'.

In 1922 a General Election was called with 'startling suddenness' and the vicar noted that the seat was unlikely to be contested in Ambleside. If there was to be a contest then everyone should 'follow the advice of the Archbishop of Canterbury and elect a fit and Godly person . . .'. At a Diocesan conference held in Hawkshead in 1919, representatives had agreed that it would not be a good idea to 'take ideas from the Labour leaders' but the magazine does not record if the same message still went out at the 1922 election.

Three notable people from Ambleside died in 1923: Mr Gatey, 'the father of Ambleside', and Miss Mason of the House of Education both died in February 1923. Mr Gatey was the person who unveiled the War Memorial and it was said of him that 'every movement in Ambleside for the past fifty years he was concerned with'. Of Miss Mason it was written that –

Her influence, her writings and her teaching have spread far and wide throughout the world: a very high rank will she take amongst the educationists of this or any other age. But that which so greatly endeared her to her students, her staff and her friends was her humble living Christian faith and character.

Sadly for Miss Mason the college she founded was not recognised by the Ministry of Education in her lifetime.

Miss Frances Arnold died aged 89,

the last survivor of the illustrious band who made our valley a shrine for the literary pilgrims of the world. No teacher from the highest to the lowest ever left her presence without receiving renewed faith and inspiration.

All her long life she walked to Rydal Church on Sunday mornings for Matins and to Ambleside church on Sunday evenings for Evensong. She took part part in movements that provided Ambleside with a District Nurse and a Clothing Club, and she was a founder member of the Girls' Friendly Club.

Albert Fleming of Neum Crag, a great supporter and patron of Brathay church also died in 1923.

To celebrate Empire Day in 1923 a 'record was procured of the King and Queen's speeches to the scholars of the Empire'; in order to be able to play the record to the children the school Governors bought a gramophone. A respondent from oral history remembered

Empire Day was on the 24th May . . . we had a flagpole in the school yard and on Empire Day we all had to form up in proper lines and march past and eyes right and salute . . .

The Band of Hope Committee from Skelwith took members children to Grange-over-Sands.

The object being to show children for the first time in their lives the sea-side, and as a side show a railway train. They noted we must remember our spades and buckets next time if that ever comes.

On New Years Day in 1924 the vicar of Ambleside noted that there had been 107″ of rainfall in Ambleside in 1923! He wanted to express his pleasure that over Christmas the

services, the bell ringers, the choir and the decorations were all perfect and he was pleased to announce the Sunday School prizes went to four outstanding girls.

His next sermon would be on

punctuality, purposefulness, patience and the danger of procrastination.

He was also pleased to state that the Girl Guides, which had been started in Ambleside in 1918 with 25 Guides now mustered 159 including the Brownies.

The League of Nations

The formation of the League of Nations in 1919 was part of the Treaty of Versailles, and as such was greeted with enthusiasm throughout Britain. Lectures were given locally on the League as reported in the magazine

we have no doubt the subject will attract the thinking sort of our men . . . it is pure, splendid practical Christianity.

Mr Hough of White Crags, owner of one of the big houses, gave a garden fête in connection with the League of Nations *probably the largest meeting ever held in the Parish. It started at 7.p.m. and went on till midnight; speakers included the Labour Member for Wrexham, the local Member of Parliament Colonel Weston, and the Bishop of Carlisle.*

By 1923 the formation of The League of Nations had struck a deep chord in the parishes, and under the headline 'The League of Nations for Church and Home', the vicar wrote . . .

the League is the greatest philanthropic society which the world has ever seen. But let the Church stand aloof and the Church will suffer no less than the League.

There were now 52 member states and the question asked was should Abyssinia stay in while she still 'slave-raids?' The Irish Free State had applied and 'amid applause was admitted though no longer part of the British Empire'. A Sunday had been dedicated as World Peace Sunday when sermons should be preached in every Church throughout the land on the League and

Peace on Earth. The first duty of the League is to keep the peace of the world and it must have public opinion behind it.

On Armistice Day in Ambleside in 1925 the vicar wrote:

we must surely see better the monstrous folly and wickedness of nations attempting to settle disputes by war . . . no single nation is the better for it . . . it is a matter if great thankfulness that the Pact which has just been agreed at Locarno gives a better hope of peace for the world.

The pact the vicar was referring to was signed in 1925: it was a pact of non-aggression between France, Germany and Belgium, and guaranteed by Britain and Italy. A. J. P. Taylor writes:

From the British point of view Locarno marked the moment when Great Britain regarded the European responsibilities as discharged.

Governments believed they had established peace in Europe for ever.

During the Armistice Day Sunday service a collection was taken for Earl Haigs Fund

to relieve the great distress which still exists among the unemployed ex-servicemen of all ranks. The Ambleside Charity Trustees have at their disposal a sum of money from which grants may be made to help sons of ex-servicemen make a start in life. Information from the Vicar. Wherever you are and whatever you are doing observe the two minutes reverential silence in grateful remembrance of Englands sacrifices.

In 1926 Canon and Mrs Irving visited the great Cathedral at Amiens where they saw the

carved oak Cross dedicated to the men of Hawkshead and Lindale . . . who gave their lives.

The Cathedral was

sacred to the memory of 600,000 of the Armies of Great Britain and Ireland who fell in France and Belgium during the Great War of 1914-1918. In this Diocese lie their dead of the Battle of the Somme 1916, the Defence of Amiens in 1916 and the March to Victory in 1918.

Canon and Mrs Irving sent flowers all the mothers and widows from Hawkshead who had lost sons and husbands in the war.

It was on November 11th 1928 that doubts about the future of Europe were raised by the vicar though he did not clarify the grounds for his pessimism.

The sacrifices which were then made would have been worth while if results had been obtained worthy of the ideals for which many did sacrifice their all. But nobody can look on the state of Europe today and feel this is so.

The League of Nations still had wide Church support with a special League of Nations Sunday set aside. The local branch of the League held its annual general meeting in the Hawkshead Town Hall where the speaker made 'shrewd and convincing comments on H. G. Well's' recent criticism of the League'. There was a rally of all the North Lancashire Branches which was held at Holker Hall where Viscount Cecil spoke to an enthusiastic gathering.

A Disarmament Conference of 'immense importance' was held in 1932; 'the growth of armaments was one of the contributory causes of the Great War'. The vicar noted that

by signing the Kellogg Pact in 1928 all nations have renounced war as a means of settling disputes. The civilised world is in a very serious state; many nations are crushed under a heavy burden of debt which some are quite unable to pay, of taxes that are making them poorer, and of unemployment because other nations cannot or will not buy their goods. The problem is finding employment for thousands of men who are sick at heart for want of any settled means of livelihood.

The vicar of Hawkshead echoed the sentiment . . .

if we allow ourselves to be unduly frightened by the gloomy forecasts concerning the future . . . we must pin our hopes on the forthcoming international conference on War debt, reparations and disarmament.

A Day of Prayer was set aside on 3rd January 1932, and an international conference on disarmament, war debt and reparations was arranged for February 1932.

On League of Nations Sunday in August 1932 the Vicar of Hawkshead asked the parishioners to

pray for the day when fear and suspicion, with war as an inevitable sequel, will cease and international goodwill and peace be firmly established.

The League took the moral position that peace should be maintained through collective security not war: there was no peace keeping force, and the only weapon was the imposition of sanctions. The first challenge came in 1931 when Japan invaded Manchuria, and the League was helpless. In 1935 the Italians under General Mussolini invaded Abyssinia, and in 1936 Hitler marched into the demilitarised Rhineland. Britain and France were powerless, and according to A. J. P. Taylor, public opinion was against any military action. In 1938 Germany invaded Czechoslovakia, and the League ceased to be a force to be reckoned with.

Unemployment

The Council did not seem to think unemployment was a problem within the township. In 1921 they recorded that

> there were only 33 unemployed in Ambleside, mostly young men engaged in seasonal work, and this from a population of around 2500.

The church seemed to have a deeper understanding of the problem. In 1923 the number of unemployed men was rising locally; and the solution offered by the church was the same as it had been in the 1880s, which was for families to consider emigration. A promise was made that emigrants to Australia would be helped

> by the Church Army who try and get families adopted by Australian parishes. All war funds for helping the ex-soldier and his family to migrate are closed down . . . many of the men and their families are impoverished for want of work . . . the Church hopes to be able to make small grants towards passages, and equipment for starting up, and they may be able to lend money.

In Hawkshead the vicar was urging parishioners to consider emigrating to Canada. Although Canon Irving had a sympathetic approach to families considering emigration, his attitude towards the unemployed men was the opposite. He wrote in June 1924.

> One of the many disturbing signs of the times is the dislike so widely shown of work, with strong and able men preferring the 'dole'. Men now start work at 8 a.m.! Work must be the slogan, and in your holidays do some useful work – perhaps some manual labour.

The vicar deplored the 'futility' of the miners strike which started in 1926, and felt he must comment on its continuation.

> The dispute in the coal industry has led to a decrease in the countrys prosperity and that has naturally made itself felt here . . . warfare in industry is as miserable and evil as warfare between nations.

What was needed was a strong moral code because 'all sin comes from lack of self-control'. The vicar went on:

> In the newspaper today there was an account of seven couples getting divorced, there was a murder of a sweetheart, and there was an account of a libel action. All these

three are examples of the effect of passions unrestrained and evil desires unchecked. Many homes are made miserable by such actions and . . . we must learn to resist temptation.

The solution lay with 'Prayer and Fasting and Almsgiving'. To add to every ones woes there had been a run of bad harvests which affected the root crops as well as the corn.

By the end of the decade the plight of the miners was demanding a response: the Christmas collection at Brathay Church raised £11. 14s. 11d and was given to the Miners Coal Distress Fund, and the Church at Sawrey, now in the magazine consortium, raised £14. 2s. 6d. by giving a gramophone recital. But the congregation did more than send money; they reacted as they had done during the war and started sewing. Brathay parish was able to send garments to west Cumberland through the Ambleside Police, and they duly received thanks from the Mayor of Workington. A further parcel of clothes was sent to the miners families in Aberdare in South Wales.

Unemployment continued to rise and in 1931 there were over 3,000,000 people out of work. When unemployment benefit was first introduced it was initially only for a few selected trades, but during the war munition workers gained cover. In 1920 unemployment insurance was extended to cover virtually all working people except agricultural labourers, and allowances were made for a wife and children. The principle of insurance cut across the the Adam Smith concepts of laisser faire, and it also cut across the old principles of the Poor Law because insurance did not have the element of humiliation attached to it. Men were no longer driven to look for work for wages lower than they would get from the public assistance rates. In 1928 the old Board of Guardians was abolished and their place was taken by new Public Assistance Committees which were run by the Local Authorities.

In the magazine written on January 1st, 1931 the vicar wrote:

This year opens with our Country in a very serious state, with widespread unemployment and much depression in all trades, and with heavy taxation chiefly due to the immense debt which we contracted during the Great War. The economy is not going to be the only cure for our present troubles, but it is one ingredient of a cure. We must get rid the sin and misery and destitution with which England is afflicted today.

In September that year the vicar wrote:

The Country is faced with great danger and the foreign observer is loosing confidence in England with the result our credit has been going down . . . there is so much unemployment and bad trade, and if we go on paying unemployment benefit at the rate we have done we shall be unable to make our income equal to our expenses which is what balancing the budget means. The pound sterling will loose value and now stands at 25 French francs to the pound, whereas in 1926 there were 250 French francs to the pound. If the pound fell half as much as the franc it would mean that 1lb of bacon which can now be bought for 1/- would cost 5/-.

Income tax rose in 1931 from 4/- to 5/-.

By October the situation was if anything worse, and the vicar expressed that in his opinion because the value of the £1 was now 10/- there was a real emergency, but

church people must co-operate with our King and his Government in whatever steps are decided on.

The following month there was a general election, and the vicar predicted that the new Government was going to

reduce unemployment benefit, and it was to be expected that there would be cuts all round in wages and salaries, as well as new and severe demands by the Income tax people . . . it was all part of the 1914 legacy.

Following the Wall Street New York stock exchange crash of 1929 there had been a run on the pound causing a serious financial crises, and a National Government was formed in 1931. One of its first acts was to impose a 10% cut in the salaries of all state employees, including the judges, the armed services and the police. The teachers had a 15% cut in their salaries, and the unemployed also had 10% cut from their meagre allowances. In A. J. P. Taylor's view

if poverty had been the great social evil of Victorian times then unemployment now took its place,

but of course, unemployment bred the same poverty. There were hunger marches to London from Jarrow, and some politicians demanded radical solutions.

The new National Government has been formed and must take immediate remedies . . . it may have to increase taxes . . . to stop the rise in the cost of living.

The vicar of Ambleside wrote

The National Insurance Scheme and Public Assistance Committees have secured that the out of work are fed, but for clothing and boots they depend on the kindness of others, and the means of the charitable in the distressed districts are exhausted by the demands.

The Personal Service League has been formed . . . it is an organisation for collection and making of clothes and boots. The north of England, South Wales and parts of Scotland have between 40% and 60% of the population unemployed, and many have been unemployed for years. There are boys and girls with good prospects, some of whom have won scholarships, but they have no clothes. There are women who cannot go out in the daytime because the eldest daughter has to wear the boots to school. There are families in Wales where the one decent dress is shared and the daughters go to church alternate Sundays. Boots . . . the more a man is determined to find work the more boot leather he wears out.

78

A work party will be started at the vicarage but there are no funds to buy materials with.

The work party for the Personal Service League did get started and women were asked to bring their sewing machines along. Material had been donated . . .

and with the approach of winter the need for warm clothes in the distressed areas will become urgent.

The Personal Service League at Hawkshead was hoping to send off a large consignment of new clothes to Manchester, but 'gifts of old clothes will be very welcome'.

At Christmas 1932 the vicar wrote in the magazine that:

Experienced parish priests in large towns where there are many unemployed have lately testified to the fact that there are many families of which the members never get enough food really to nourish them, and of course such undernourished people have no reserve of strength to fight against illness when it attacks them . . . I do not think people realise how much semi starvation there is with plenty of decent working men tramping the country not as tramps but genuinely looking for work. However, on Christmas Day we give our annual collection to the Sick and Poor Fund and we do not have to go out of Ambleside to find poverty, unemployment and sickness. Please support us on Christmas Day.

He later noted that the number of communicants both at Ambleside and Brathay was 'the largest for many years'.

The work parties during 1933 produced almost as many garments for the poor as they had done for the men at the front during the Great War. The Hawkshead group had had £22 kindly donated, and made 440 new garments, which together with 280 second hand garments, were sent to Manchester and Stoke. In fact Hawkshead made well over 1,000 garments in the course of a year. The Women's Institute at Brathay joined in and sent nearly 400 new items to Manchester. These work parties were master minded by Lady Reading.

By November 1938 matters still had not improved. The vicar writes:

Unemployment is high in the cotton trade. In some mill towns more than half the population are out of work. The 'dole' pays the rent and provides fuel and food enough to keep body and soul together, but there is nothing left for clothing. This is an agonising problem – when our clothes drop off us in rags how are we to get new ones.

The Personal Service League distributed clothing to every part of the country, and a

branch in Ambleside is working for Lancashire. Come to Wansfell Tower, Ambleside, between 3 and 4 any Thursday afternoon bringing second hand clothing . . . men's clothing is especially needed . . . come and make a garment . . . or knit socks . . .

Employment

A respondent from the oral history archive remembered 1919.

I remember all those chaps coming back out of the army . . . there were nearly a few riots in Ulverston. There was nothing no work for them, nothing for them to do these ex-servicemen and they had a job to get something to eat . . . I went to a hiring fair at Martinmas. I could handle horses . . . I got hired for £12 for t'half year living in on a farm. Then I worked breaking stones at 5/- per cubic yard and I earned 12/6d per week.

Another respondent had a similar experience;

I went to the hiring fair in 1925 and got taken on by a farmer and I was paid £1 a week, but I had to wait six months for it. I took my clothes round with me in a tin box . . . the farmers wife did the washing and mending and cooking for us . . .

The wages paid to the farm labourers was a little better than the wages paid before the war. This respondent, born in 1891, described being hired in 1905.

. . . and I hired with this farmer and my pay was £6. 10s for six months and I'd no money . . . he wanted me to start right away the chap I hired with. No I said . . . and I went to Graythwaite Hall pheasant beating and I got 3s. a day for four days, I got 12s. . . . I wanted a new pair of boots and I walked six miles to Hawkshead and bought a pair which cost 7s. 6d. . . . and I'd 4s. 6d. to last me

Haymaking is hard work.

six months and it did do. At my second hiring when I was 18 I got £11 for six months. If you left within that time you couldn't claim your money.

In 1919 the wages paid by Ambleside Urban District Council to roadmen were 47/6d per week for a 48 hour week in the four winter months, and the same for a 52 hour week for the eight summer months. The Foreman was paid 50/- a week, and engine drivers 55/- a week. In 1921 the Westmorland Industrial Council resolved a reduction of workmens wages by nearly 1d. an hour because the cost of living was falling. This was a very good wage compared to the agricultural labourers wages. An apprentice boot maker earned 3/6d a week through his time . . .

There was work in the area but it was often hard, with long hours and poor wages, it could be humiliating, and it could be dangerous; but there was work to be found for the young in domestic service. A teacher commenting in an oral history tape said –

There was no shortage of jobs because the big houses were all in occupation of the cotton magnates and maids were always wanted. They might have a staff of seven or a dozen even, parlour maids, house parlour maids, a cook and a housekeeper. Many housewives in the village worked . . . girls didn't expect anything else . . . but they could become dressmakers or drapers or something like that . . . the boys often went to Barrow to the ship yards to look for work . . .

It was said with great authority by one respondent that before the first world war the le Flemmings of Rydal Hall employed 32 staff to look after them and their four children. This number included governesses, a French governess, a nannie and an under nannie as well a butler, footmen and maids. It is unlikely the numbers would remain at that level post war. At Holehird, the home of the Leigh Groves in the 1930s, there was a staff of 25 including the maids, under-maids, scullery maids who lived in, and the chauffeurs, grooms and gardeners who lived in staff cottages. The number of gardeners was particularly large because the owners grew orchids, peaches, nectarines, cactus and bananas, and they employed one individual gardener for every greenhouse. Keeping the temperatures even in the glass houses was demanding; 'if you lost your job you lost your home'.

There is no doubt there was considerable exploitation of young girls by the middle class or upper class people, frequently referred to as 'the gentry.' One of the more disgraceful stories from the oral history archives was told by a daughter of the head gardener to one of the big houses:

Lady Holt was a Governor of an orphanage in Manchester and she used to get her servants from the orphanage, and they had to stop a year and then they got a black dress. The servants were very poor. They only had to go to church on Sunday morning. They didn't get a day off or an afternoon off or anything. They worked and worked. They would get 2/6d. a week. They had a poor do, you know, those poor orphans.

It was not only the girls that went to work for the gentry in the big houses, as this man told in his story.

I left school in 1934 in the depression . . . they didn't want to take anybody on . . . people were cutting staff. I became an apprenticed gardener . . . the big houses wanted their gardens remodelling with fancy ornamental trees and all that . . . all the estates had gardeners . . . some up to five . . . an awful lot of people worked as gardeners – even small houses kept a gardener.

There was no doubt the wealthy owners of the large houses created employment;

my mother did washing for the gentry . . . all the aprons from the big houses what the maids wore they all had to be starched and the little caps and collars had to be starched and the frills had to be goffered . . .

At Christmas my mother couldn't afford toys because half the time my father was out of work. You might get an apple or an orange or a sugar mouse . . . My mother used to buy lights from the butcher . . . you'd give that to dogs now . . .

When I was 14 I was a house parlour maid. I used to have to wait on. My mistress insisted I went to the Anglican church even though I was a Methodist, and she insisted I got confirmed. I hadn't got a white dress, and I was made to wear her old tennis dress. All the other girls they all had lovely white dresses and I had on this blinking tennis dress . . .

Describing her work in one of the big houses in 1929, when employed as a maid at the age of 15, the following respondent was very articulate.

You got up at half past six, you'd all the front steps to scrub and you had the stairs, there was miles of them carpeted of course . . . you'd got to be doing them by 7 o'clock . . . you didn't speak out of turn you know. After lunch you'd all the darning, and mending sheets . . . after tea post time . . . dinner at 8 o'clock which was about eight courses . . . you didn't finish till ten o'clock. I had Thursday afternoon off, after I had cleared lunch. You had to be in by ten o'clock. Sunday mornings you'd got to go to church and you must sit in front of the ladies so they'd know you were in church. I got paid £20 a year, and I was paid £5 a quarter. A coat cost £2 and a pair of new shoes 12/6d. Sometimes we had titled people on their way to Scotland; they'd be going to their shooting lodges. They would stay with their entourage of chauffeurs, ladies maids and what have you . . . a bigger nuisance to us than the gentry . . . they took a lot of looking after . . . their servants shared our servants hall.

My eldest sister had been working in the paper mill . . . she had real long hair and it get caught in the machine and you know in those days they weren't so fussy about regulations . . . she was very injured . . . there was no compensation.

Another man was almost disembowelled working in the bobbin mill, and described vividly the dangers of unfenced machinery.

Almost eighty years previously in the 1840s Charles Dickens and Harriet Martineau had a passionate difference of opinion about 'meddlesome

Girls hard at work in the Horrax Laundry, Stock Ghyll.

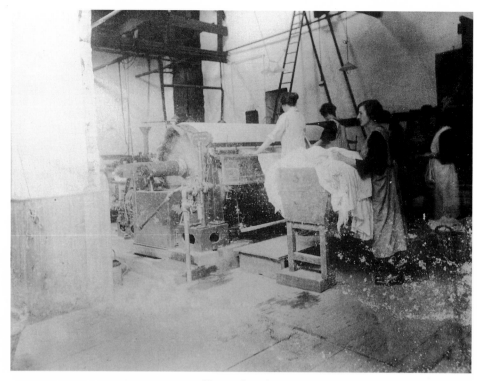

Horrax Laundry.

legislation' contained in the Factory Acts. Martineau 'as a manufacturers daughter' was against state interference and wrote a pamphlet on the subject: Dickens, on the other hand was in favour of protection for workers. He wrote an article for '*Household Words*' about operatives who had been drawn into machines and 'slain by every variety of torture . . . '. In reply to the Martineau publication he suggested an organisation might be started called 'The National Association for the Protection of the Right to Mangle Operatives', and said of Martineau 'I do not suppose there was ever such a wrong headed woman born – such a vain one or such a humbug'. Factory Inspectors had been in existence long before the 1920s but there was not enough of them, and it would appear that their recommendations or advice regarding the protection of dangerous machinery could be ignored with impunity.

Leisure and Tourism

The church had always through the magazine expressed strong ideas on what was or was not acceptable as a leisure pursuit, and what was or was not seemly behaviour. One legacy from the war was the increasing popularity of the gramophone, and with the introduction of the new type of dancing like the Charleston, the loosening of the controls became inevitable.

The vicar of Brathay wrote:

the young amongst us crave for amusement and show indifference to religious exercises.

This sentiment was echoed by Canon Irving.

We wish there was less dancing on Saturday evenings . . . it is an unwholesome preparation for Sabbath worship and rest . . .

Herbert Bell, the renowned local photographer gave a lecture on 'Old Ambleside' which was perfectly acceptable, but dancing, it appears, was not. It was described as

careless, frivolous, and forgetful . . . they dance on the rim of decadence whilst the Eastern (yellow and brown) Nations watch their chance – and then – chaos . . .

On the rim of decadence or not dancing had became extremely popular by the 1930s.

There was the Fire Brigade Dance, the Ambulance Dance, the Rugby Club dance and the Hunt Ball. They started at 8 p.m. and ended at 3 a.m . . . and cost 2/6d or 3/6d. . . . and you got a good dinner. You daren't go unless you'd a suit on, and you'd got to wear gloves . . . all the women wore gloves . . and the men had dancing shoes. The big balls were absolutely packed . . . and you'd be thrown out if you were unsteady 'cos you'd had a drink.

One respondent gave an interesting insight into the class structure of the time.

There were three classes of people at the dances, probably the Redmaynes and the people from Loughrigg Brow would be there all at the top against the orchestra . . . then there were the farmers and such like, and down at the very bottom of the room was what they called the laundry clique, a lot of girls from the laundry . . .

Leisure activities included bell ringing, and the church had two teams of ringers, there were two brass bands, a choral society, an operatic society, and

some times in the Assembly rooms there would be a social evening with piano playing, recitations, singing or a conjuror.

Canon Irving wrote:

Do lectures in winter meet a need? What about a lecture by the vicar on Charles Dickens? Many turn with disgust from the poor washy stuff of the present to Dickens.

'Amusement is good', wrote the vicar, and has its place, but a 'plethora of whist drives is certainly not good'.

Canon Irving deplored the 'vulgar din and devilry of the bookies' and pleaded for the powers that be to

eliminate the betting element at the races and there is still a chance for decent sport . . . otherwise in a short time only twisters will be left and it will be good-bye to decency. Gambling and Sport are two distinct things: they are opposed.

The vicar of Langdale was also implacably opposed to gambling.

Hundreds and thousands of happy homes have been wrecked through this pleasurable excitement, this desire to make money quickly, this selfish, everyman for himself 'sport' which takes such full advantage of a man's weakness without regard for the poverty of his home or sickness of wife and child. I know nothing more unutterably selfish than the fever of gambling.

A month or so later he wrote again on the same theme,

there is a gulf fixed by the careless, the indifferent, the gamblers, betting men, swearers, Sunday breakers and the downright vicious. A Christian is a marked man . . . there is a gulf fixed by other members of family or other workers.

In 1926 Lancashire County Library opened a small branch in both Skelwith and Hawkshead elementary schools. Canon Irving did not approve because he did not think the library service should be free. 'All borrowers should be charged at least a halfpenny instead of the ratepayer'. In his opinion

education all round at huge expense is being bungled . . . all sorts of fads have been tried . . . the real foundation has been skimped . . . not 10% have really learnt to read a book . . .

However, the vicar of Brathay was more generous in his praise,

this library ought to be a great acquisition to the neighbourhood chiefly because the supply of books will be both modern and constantly changed.

There was some coming together over the class divide when it came to sport. This respondent remembers

Cricket . . . the wealthy people from the big houses played cricket with us . . . they played cricket in July and August when they broke up from their public schools or universities . . . The Squire of Rydal played cricket, and the Redmaynes from Brathay Hall, and some of them played rugger with us . . . Bathing was popular with visitors, but bathing in the lake ended because there were so many tin cans floating down, we were living in the tin can age, and there were thousands of cans and people cutting their feet it got really bad. So they decided to close it down . . . in the 1950s.

In 1930 the Urban District Council was asked by the National Flying Services about any plans they may have for an aerodrome, but their reply is not on record. Meanwhile, after a lot of hard work on the slopes of Loughrigg, Ambleside golf course opened in 1931. It was minuted that the

Ladies and Gentleman Captain be invited by the Council to play off the first ball, and that the Town Band be invited to play during the evening.

Tourism continued to give Ambleside its life blood, and the number of small hotels and boarding houses grew. During the 1920s and 1930s in spite of the countrys economic woes, if people were in work they were relatively prosperous because the cost of living was falling, and the Council did its best to advertise

Ambleside. The concept of a weeks holiday away from home was spreading to the weekly wage earner and the less well off. 'Farming was so poor you had to depend on visitors', said one respondent who came from three generations of hoteliers, and farm holidays became fashionable.

But perhaps not everyone was made welcome.

At first it was the very wealthy that came – only the very wealthy could afford it. And then we had the artists, doctors, bishops, writers . . . and Sir William Beveridge . . . all sorts of interesting people. Then buses and charabancs went up Langdale. We'd never met buses before! But they came to New Dungeon Ghyll and we hated them. These people came, they used to drink beer and never look at the fells . . . sometimes they brought barrels of beer on the top of their buses they just came to have a booze-up you know these men, there weren't women, it was just a booze-up . . . so we stopped the bus trade.

But life for the boarding house keeper was hard, and the holiday season short.

My mother was up by six to light the fire. Hot water was boiled in the boiler at the side of the fire so all that had to be carried through for washing up. We had to carry hot water to the bedrooms in cans, and the guests shoes had to be cleaned before breakfast. My mother cooked a large breakfast . . . then she made sandwiches for the walkers . . . then afternoon tea . . . and a proper dinner at night with a roast. We had no bathroom but there was an indoor toilet so we were better off than some. We had no electricity until 1930 . . . no gas lights in the bedrooms they had to use candles . . . and we had no telephone until 1939. The same people came every year . . . there were virtually no cars then . . . our guests came on boats, or the train or the bus. In 1930 dinner, bed and breakfast was 16/-, and full board for a week was 6 gns. We advertised in the Ambleside Guide . . .

The Magazine

On the 11th November

our beloved vicar went to sleep, on earth, in Hawkshead, on Wednesday night November 10th, and woke up on the early morning of Armistice Day, Thursday November 11th in Heaven to find his gallant son, who had laid down his life in the Great War, embracing him with an embrace of joyous welcome. It was a beautiful home-going.

Canon Irving was born in 1856. Mrs Irving died a month later in December 1926.

At Christmas that year the vicar of Ambleside wrote:

. . . there are many people who exist without one atom of thought or care for the religious aspect of Christmas and make it an occasion for self-indulgence and eating and drinking . . .

He intended the first celebration of Communion on Christmas Day should commence at 6.45 a.m. He was later able to report that the number of communicants was up on the previous year, and to provide for their needs the first service on the following Easter Sunday would be held at 6 a.m. and the second service at 6.45 a.m.

Money was needed for the Church organ, but the 'free will' offering promised to raise only £100 a year. In 1926 the Church gave £103. 5s. 0d to the Home and Foreign Missions; £59. 17s. 3d. to the Diocesan and Central funds; £119. 10s. 6d. to the Maintenance of Clergy fund and £26. 9s. 6d towards religious instruction. The church was also £23 in debt.

Langdale Parish of Holy Trinity became incorporated with the Ambleside, Brathay and Hawkshead magazine, and in 1927, the vicar of Langdale had 25 candidates for confirmation. In his first address printed in the magazine the vicar pointed out that in

less than a fortnight any ordinary cinema palace holding 300 to 500 people takes nearly double the total income of such a Church in Langdale in a whole year.

He went on to point out that half the income of the Church of England came from past endowments. The remaining half amounting to £7,000,000, which came from voluntary subscriptions, should be 'compared to £300,000,000 spent annually on alcoholic drink'.

The magazine also carried the following story under the section entitled *Missionary News:*

A Bishop in German South West Africa visited an Englishman stationed among natives miles from the nearest white man. The man was found in his shack eating his evening meal in full evening dress. 'I do it because its been what I've been used to and to remind myself I am a white man'.

The Ambleside vicar wrote the following month

there still survives among Christian the peculiar form of pride known as race superiority. Anglo-Saxons are specially liable to this infection . . . it must be cast out. There should be unity between all races and therefore the colour question should not arise.

One of the most important inventions was, of course, the wireless, and it was generally agreed to have a greater impact on the general population than the newspapers. Every household wanted to possess a wireless if it could be afforded. In 1926 the British Broadcasting Corporation was created by Royal Charter. A. J. P. Taylor writes:

Reith turned broadcasting into a mission which was to bring into every home all that was best in every department of human knowledge.

He used what Taylor called the

brute force of monopoly to stamp the Calvinist morality on the British people. He also stamped it on his employees who lost their jobs if touched by the breath of impropriety.

Ten years later in 1936 the B.B.C. broadcast evensong from St Mary's church on the Northern Wavelength –

a well deserved tribute to the choir and Mr Skelton, the choirmaster, to have reached such a high standard.

The loss of important patrons was becoming a serious problem to the church both nationally and locally because the rich were becoming poorer. As an example of patronage every Christmas the Redmaynes gave a party at Brathay Hall for the Sunday school children, but only for the good attenders, and the children received a book, an orange and 6d. After the Redmaynes left Brathay Hall the Christmas party ceased. The Sunday school attenders at Hodge Close only received a book. A major house called 'The Croft' was closing, because the owners could not afford the upkeep, and other big houses were to follow. The vicar of Brathay was complaining that the Sunday School attendance and evensong attendance were not what they used to be. On the other hand Hawkshead still had six Sunday school teachers, and Ambleside still had twelve sidesmen, plus two church wardens, an organist, a choirmaster, a choir of forty and a verger. The Band of Hope Christmas tea continued 'to be a pleasure'. The Church magazine in Hawkshead went to 180 houses and cost 2d. per month, and the number of communicants continued to rise.

There was the constant complaint about the shortage of clergy, not through lack of applicants, but from shortage of funds for training. A. J. P. Taylor in his book in his book 'English History 1914-1945' commented that following the end of the first world war there was a decline in church attendance. There were roughly speaking at this time about three million Anglicans, two and a half million Roman Catholics and about two million Dissenters or non-conformists. Taylor writes:

Religious faith was loosing its strength, and church going universally declined . . . This was as great a happening as any in English history since the conversion of the Anglo-Saxons to Christianity. It had many causes: the old rationalism of the eighteenth century; the new rationalism of science, particularly of biology . . .

Taylor conceded that if there was a decline in church attendance there was no evidence in a decline of Christian morality; standards of probity in public life remained high, a contract was a contract, and a man was as good as his word. There was evidence of discrimination against the Jews, and to a lesser extent against Roman Catholics. There was some evidence that sexual morality became more lax; it was said that in the twenties there was a more frivolous attitude towards sex outside marriage but divorce was still frowned upon. Taylor wrote, 'the Conservative Party maintained a ban on divorce until after the second world war' even though it had become legal in certain circumstances. A. P. Herbert had carried a private members bill in Parliament in 1937 which added insanity and desertion to adultery as grounds for divorce.

In September 1930, 307 Bishops met at Lambeth and issued an Encyclical Letter.

Holy marriage is part of God's plan for mankind . . . and it follows that divorce is unnatural. Therefore marriage of a divorced person in church whose former partner is living should not be allowed.

During the conference they stated that the minimum stipend for all clergy should be £420 per annum: they acknowledged the shortage of clergy, and said there were now only 15,000 clergymen whereas in 1914 there were 20,000.

The Ambleside vicar wrote in September 1932

It is true that there is a very large number of people in the country who make no open profession of religion at all. But this means that people who do profess it are all the keener.

Ambleside church at this time had three Bible study classes, one for the over sixteens, one for boys between the ages of 14 and 16 and one for girls between the ages of 14 and 16. There were also three Sunday school classes which were for senior mixed boys and girls from age 11 to 14, juniors between the age of 7 and 11, and infants. At Easter 1934 there were 494 communicants from an electoral role of 545, but these numbers could well be distorted by the number of visitors to the township. Nevertheless the local vicars could feel that at least in this part of rural England the congregations were holding up well. There was certainly no shortage of evangelical zeal.

The Langdale contribution to the combined parish Church magazine ceased early in 1928, and in the last edition the vicar urged the readers to

beware of the advocates of Evolution who refuse to accept Biblical statements . . .

He wanted people also to remember that

men go to the Devil through drink.

In spite of the unemployment and general economic gloom, the church continued to demand month on month, money for a variety of good causes. There were the foreign Missions, and Missionaries received little remuneration, 'they left this country to serve the heathen brethren', and a constant plea went out that the Missions were failing from lack of financial support. Mr Hough of 'White Craggs' held a big garden party and sale in aid of the missionary training school at Warminster.

Ambleside Nursing Association was trying to organise a pension for Nurse Deacon so that when she retired there would be some recognition of her devoted work of 16 years.

Hawkshead was trying to raise funds for the Town Hall and even put in central heating.

The annual collection for Kendal Hospital remained essential.

In September 1929 an appeal by the Bishop of Carlisle went out for £5,000 to modernise Church schools –

> . . . *many of the schools are substandard in sanitary arrangements, play grounds etc. This modern standard is insisted on by the Board of Education, and if the Church is not able to keep the schools up to it they are taken over by the State and become Council schools. In such schools there can be no definite Church teaching at all, and the children of Church parents are thus deprived of the privilege of being taught their faith.*

The running expenses of Ambleside church continued to cause concern as they amounted to between £350 and £400 per annum. This sum included the cost of repairs to the fabric of the building as well as the cost of cleaning the church and churchyard, where a man was employed full time. On top of that there were the salaries of both the organist and the choirmaster, the rewards for the choir boys, the insurance costs, and the on going cost of St Anne's church.

The congregation remained good, but evidently needed the reminder that

> *no person should fail to come to Church on Good Friday, especially when that day is so profaned by merrymaking and drunkenness . . .*

In January 1931 the vicar of Brathay reported that . . .

> *high revels were held at Skelwith, the occasion being the annual New Year gathering of the Band of Hope. The attendance tested to the utmost the available accommodation.*

At the Vestry meeting at Hawkshead church it was decided 'to install a small petrol engine to blow the organ.' Later there were to be complaints about the petrol engine, the 'blowing apparatus', which 'smelt of petrol which is unpleasantly strong at times'.

In July 1929 the landscape painter Alfred Heaton Cooper died without an obituary from the vicar. However, the vicar did observe that there was going to be a meeting on the 'Preservation of the Lake District'. 'We must guard against ugliness'. The public meeting was organised by the National Conference for the Preservation of the Countryside, and would be held in the Queens Hotel Pavilion, Ambleside.

In February 1933 it was recorded that Doctor Parsons had died; Doctor Parsons was the general practitioner to John Ruskin and had always attended to him on horseback. Later that year the death was recorded of Mr John Purdom, aged 83, 'plant collector extraordinary'. Mr Purdom was the eldest son of the head gardener at Brathay Hall and had the good fortune to go to Kew gardens for training. He later went to Tibet where he sent back seeds of rare specimen trees and plants to White Craggs, the home of Dr Hough and his daughters, where they were planted and flourished.

In November 1934 Ambleside Parish Magazine published an article by J. B. Priestley, which first appeared in the *London Evening Standard*, called 'The Lost Generation'.

> *And the men that were boys when I was a boy will sit and drink with me; thus the*

poet. I hope he is luckier than I am. Most of the men who were boys when I was a boy cannot sit and drink with me. Loos and Gallipoli and the Somme did for them. They went out and saved something and never came back. What it was they saved I cannot exactly tell but I do know that I have never seen anything since 1918 that was worth their sacrifice.

I celebrated my 21st birthday in 1915 on the front line . . . the finest members of my generation were lost to us through the war.

I doubt if you can grow to manhood under such circumstances – if you can spend the most impressionable years of your life among shells and bloodstained wire and be quite normal. There are wounds to the soul as well as wounds to the body . . . My generation missed normality: it spent that period watching its dearest friends being killed.

Education

During the 1930s there was little or no enthusiasm for education reform, but even so some achievements were noted: there were fewer classes of over sixty pupils in primary schools, but no real increase in numbers staying on at school after the leaving age of 14. University provision was almost stagnant, and A. J. P. Taylor pointed out that 'out of every one thousand children at an elementary school only four managed to reach university'. This division of school children between those who attended schools run by the state and those who attended private schools reinforced class distinctions, and these class distinctions remained throughout life, thereby perpetuating Disraeli's two nations.

However, there was some debate on the problems of funding education reform, though Cruikshank reports that deep divisions remained within Anglican circles, and these divisions were essentially the same as confronted the churches in 1902. Church schools wanted to provide compulsory religious education not only in their schools but also to provide religious instruction in the Council schools. The Hyde report brought new problems because the proposed secondary schools would cater for an amalgamation of several parish schools and the parish priest would there by loose control. The report floated the ideas of both giving all children secondary education and raising the school leaving age to 15. The Labour Government of 1929 endorsed this principle, but the question of who was going to pay for the new schools was impossible to solve. The churches could not afford it, and they did not want to give up control of their schools. Some voices were raised to suggest that by raising the school leaving age to 15 it would both take numbers off those unemployed, and perhaps equip the children better for the employment market.

The vicar of Ambleside conceded that although the financial slump of 1929-1934 put decisions on education spending on one side, sooner or later the church would have to come to terms with the new demands. One of the new demands was that elementary education would be divided into three parts; the infants school for those aged 5-7, the juniors for the ages 7-11, and the seniors for pupils aged 12-15. The vicar put three questions in the magazine for the parishioners:

Firstly, will we help the Church build a senior school in Ambleside sharing costs with Grasmere and Langdale? There will be approximately 120 children, the cost will be about £5,000, a grant would be given by the Board of Education for £3,700 leaving £1,250 to be found. Secondly, will we help the church build a secondary school at say Troutbeck Bridge for the whole area sharing costs? These costs would be £10,000 with £7,500 found by the Board of Education. (£1,000 has been promised by the Rural Dean so therefore only £1,500 will have to be found.) Or thirdly, should we leave the whole matter to Westmorland County Council and pay for it out of the rates?

The vicar strongly recommended the first option.

By 1938 the local church schools had more problems because they found 'they will need an assembly hall to seat 200, and they will need more class rooms'. However, the school managers still wanted to keep Ambleside senior pupils in Ambleside, and they intended to hold a public meeting to put the matter before the people.

The Education Act of 1938 wanted a separate senior school for pupils. The vicar and the school managers thought they could work out a compromise by altering the girls' school to a senior mixed school for 160 pupils. .

Whether the Authorities will accept the plan even with modifications of their own is somewhat doubtful. The cry seems to be for new schools and thousands of pounds spent on these flashy buildings while perfectly good schools are left derelict. The average cost of a senior school for 160 is £12,500 exclusive of site which must include several acres of playing fields. We can alter the girls' school for £3,000.

Perhaps to the surprise of the vicar and school managers Westmorland Education Authority agreed to turn the girls' school into a senior mixed school for the older scholars of Ambleside, Grasmere and Langdale. The Council would give a grant of 75% towards costs leaving the church to find 25%. One new provision would be a school hall, a properly equipped kitchen for school meals and domestic science lessons, and a 'practical' room for boy's carpentry and metal work. The school would also need a garden. The boys' school, set up under the Kelsick foundation 200 years ago, would loose its separate identity and become a mixed junior school. 'There was no option as under the Education Act of 1936 schools had to reorganise on an age basis instead of sex'. There were not enough children in the area for separate schools which the church preferred. The outbreak of war put school reorganisation on hold again, and it was not until the implication of the 1944 Education Act that secondary schooling for all became a reality.

The out break of war, according to Cruikshank,

brought to light the squalor and ignorance' of the evacuees; education had failed many, and a belief was expressed that inequalities and anomalies had to be eliminated and full scope given to ability wherever it existed.

In 1939 half the schools in the country were still church schools but their organisation and amenities were far behind the standards of Council schools. Separate senior schools now existed for 62% of Council schools but only 16% of church schools provided senior schools. It also came to light that 90% of all non-provided schools were built before 1902 (and certainly the Ambleside schools came into that figure). The Board of Education had a black list which included 541 voluntary schools compared to 212 Council schools.

Lakes Urban District Council

On the 31st March 1935 Ambleside Urban District Council ceased to exist and the new Lakes Urban District Council took over the Townships of Ambleside, Grasmere, Troutbeck, the Langdales and Patterdale. Minutes were still transcribed in copperplate hand writing and though the area covered was larger, the same format still pertained. A motion was put before the Committee that with a

view to relieving unemployment the Highway Committee be requested to consider the expediting of any works proposed to be undertaken by that committee.

A circular was received in July 1935 regarding future air raid precautions which the council decided they could safely ignore.

On the question of housing in Ambleside the committee again deferred any decision. Under the Housing Act of 1930 the Council had powers to demolish houses unfit for human habitation. There were six cottages in Grasmere that were condemned, and a demolition order was put on the cottages built in the yard of a well known public house called 'The Golden Rule', but 'no action could be taken until the necessary alternative accommodation was available'. The Westmorland Federation of Women's Institutes wrote to the Council with

regard to Housing and the appointment of women to serve on the Housing Committee: the Council resolved no action be taken.

A further question that was discussed in 1937 was

should the Westmorland and District Electricity Supply Co. Ltd. meet the subcommittee to discuss the electricity supply being extended to Patterdale? And should they be put into telephonic communication?

In 1938 although the Council proclaimed that

they were not aware of any nuisance caused by the existing facilities for sewerage and sewage disposal, they did resolve that the Sanitary Inspectors be instructed to consider the mode of removal of pail closet refuse and report back to the committee. The Health Committee also resolved that the Chairman of the Health Committee be authorised to make a public appeal for subscriptions for the purchase of a motor ambulance.

In September 1938 gas masks were issued, and pails of dry sand and shovels were issued to all the schools; plans from the Government on the evacuation scheme were read, and in 1939 the first evacuees were received from Newcastle and South Shields, and immediately an appeal went out for decent shoes and clothing.

The Magazine

In 1936 a new vicar the Reverend H. A. Thompson took over from Mr Selby-Luard who had been posted to Troutbeck church. The year began with the death of King George V, and a long article was written by the vicar which started 'Edward VIII surely the most gracious of our gracious Kings, was born in 1894 . . .'.

The Council sent an Address of Condolence which was forwarded to the new King which spoke of the 'irreparable loss the Nation and Empire had sustained by the death of his late Majesty'.

The Chairman of the Council and all officials went to the Market Cross in Ambleside and read the following proclamation:

Whereas it hath pleased Almighty God to call to his mercy our late Sovereign Lord King George of Blessed and Glorious Memory by whose decease the Imperial Crown of Great Britain, Ireland and all other Dominions is solely and rightfully come to the High and Mighty Prince Edward Albert Christian George Andrew Patrick David. We, therefore the Lords Spiritual and Temporal publish and proclaim that Edward the Eighth . . . to whom we acknowledge our faith and constant obedience . . .

The proclamation was read at Grasmere, in Grasmere school, and at Elterwater, Troutbeck and Patterdale.

Mr Thompson had no private means and wrote:

the upkeep of the vicarage must always have been a drain . . . it is a burden quite beyond bearing . . . a sale of work must be organised for repairs to both house and garden.

In fact he wanted to sell the vicarage.

On November 11th, 1936 the church of St Mary's was able to receive 'by Wireless' the service from the Cenotaph. The following year on the occasion of the Coronation of King George VI, the congregation had the service from the Abbey relayed into church.

Mr Thompson was an evangelist like his predecessors; his concern was – 'the need for the congregation to overcome all imperfection'. The number of communicants continued to increase, and at Easter 1938 'there were over 500'.

Mr Thompson placed the following rhyme in the magazine:

I slept and dreamed that Life was beauty
I woke and found that Life was duty.

In 1938 a strong denial was issued in the magazine that

the Ecclesiastical Commissioners owned slum property. 'As landlords they have nothing to hide and do not fear comparison in any report with any owner public or private in the country . . .

In December of that year

Sunday schools must be attended and pressure must be brought to bear by parents. Senior children between the ages of 11-15 will meet in the morning but a class will be held at 2 p.m. if pupils cannot attend morning classes.

In February 1939 he wrote

Lent calls for a curtailment of pleasure . . . There is at this time slackness, and carelessness and self-indulgence.

The church magazine, the vicar reported, now went to 'well over 400 homes'.

There was little written in the magazine in 1939 about the fact that Britain was again facing the prospect of going to war with Germany. However, Mr Thompson mentioned in the magazine

In connection with the Lord Baldwin fund for Refugees . . . there will be a nationwide appeal to the mothers of the nation on Saturday 13th May to be known as Mothers day. The purpose is to bring another 1,000 children, 500 Christians and 500 Jews out of Greater Germany. They will be given temporary homes in England until trained and ready for emigration . . . A house to house collection will be arranged . . .

A national daily paper wrote 'that churches should be used for billeting purposes in time of emergency'.

The vicar in his monthly letter in the magazine concentrated on the forthcoming Lambeth conference. Financial matters were obviously giving concern to the church and in July 1939 he wrote:

The moment a Clergyman dies his official income ceases and within two months his widow must leave the vicarage. Every effort must now be made to create a pension fund and a national appeal must be launched.

A matter to be proud of, wrote the vicar, was

the vast growth of the Anglican Communion during the first 40 years of this century. There had been enormous growth of Native Ministries even among the most unpromising races . . . an Aborigine had been ordained as Deacon, there were Eskimo priests . . . 395 ordained in East Africa, 203 in West Africa, 716 Indians, 283 Chinese, 225 Japanese . . . and a mass movement of Jews towards Christianity.

In September 1939 war against Germany was declared: the prayer went up

that now we are fighting again that truth and good faith and honour might rule among nations instead of force and lying and bad faith and dishonour.

CHAPTER FOUR

'Great Dangers Reside within Prosperity'

Church Magazine

Following the out break of war in September 1939 a Day of Prayer was fixed for the 1st of October. The government ordered that gas masks, in their cardboard boxes, were to be carried everywhere by everyone; a total blackout of all windows was imposed and the blackout also meant all street lighting was extinguished, and cars were forbidden to drive at night using headlights. (Later in the war this was modified to a heavily dipped filter light being allowed.) Perhaps the greatest upheaval was a Government initiative for the mass evacuation of school children from London and the big cities which caused great distress to both the children and the hosts. A lot of the children were ill-equipped for the countryside without warm clothing or boots; many children were verminous. It was the duty of the local authorities to organise care, but after a few months without signs of war, many children returned home. Food ration books were issued, and a register for military service was made compulsory.

The church like everyone else in the country had problems adapting to the effects of war; one great problem was because the windows of the church could not be blacked out, evensong had to start at 3 p.m. This was not a success and the vicar looked forward to the clocks going forward to summer time which was planned for the month of February.

The first six months of the war were relatively quiet, and at Easter 1940 the visitor numbers were 'not below usual'. Confirmation classes were held as usual, and an appeal sent out 'because St Anne's church needs saving from ruin'.

It was reported that because it was wartime there would be no major changes to the education system – but it was noted that repairs were necessary to the boys' school. The Kelsick Governors decided 'the school needed a new cloakroom, accommodation and offices for the staff, and provision of electric light'. Electricity had been laid on to many of the public buildings by 1940, so the vicar was able to give a public lecture with lantern slides on the life of David Livingstone. The magazine reported that 'the vicar manipulated the lantern slides while his wife read extracts on every picture'.

In April 1940 the Germans invaded both Denmark and Norway, and Britain lost control of the north sea: this, of course, created a sense of crisis in

Parliament. Following a bitter critical debate on Neville Chamberlain's premiership the House divided following an impassioned speech by a member of Parliament called Leo Amery, who ended his speech with Cromwell's words to the Rump:

Depart, I say, and let us have done with you. In the name of God, go.

Chamberlain then resigned and Winston Churchill became Prime Minister in May 1940.

In June Germany invaded Holland and Belgium, meeting little resistance, and the British army had to be evacuated from Dunkirk. Following the fall of France, when Britain stood alone, Winston Churchill broadcast his message to the people that

we shall fight on the beaches . . . we shall never surrender. Let us therefore brace ourselves to our duties, and so bear ourselves that, if the British Empire and its Commonwealth last for a thousand years, men will still say: "This was their finest hour".

The vicar was obviously deeply influenced both by the wireless broadcasts made by the Prime Minister, and by the dire news from Europe.

Events are bringing rapidly nearer the danger of which the Prime Minister warned us – the extension of the war to this island. It is not my province to discuss the whys and wherefores, but I say unto you danger will come out a clear sky . . . I am concerned about the spiritual side . . . we must stand fast . . . dawn will surely come.

I want you to take necessary action to prepare yourself because there will be no warning. We should all carry out carefully and promptly the instructions that are issued from time to time by radio.

The German threat is aimed at all we stand for our religion, our national institution, our way of life . . . we must defend them with all our powers.

After the fall of France in June 1940 the vicar wrote:

weakness among the French shows what comes of a spirit that is wanting in resolution and determination. Public worship, he said, *is a tremendous tonic. This is a war of nerves and the steadiest nerves will win.*

According to A. J. P. Taylor it was on July 16th that Hitler directed that preparations should go forward for the invasion of Britain. In order to prepare the way the German air force flew sorties day after day to try to smash both the British air force and the airfields. The battle of Britain was fought in the air over the skies of southern England, with serious losses to both sides. 'By 17th September', Taylor wrote, 'Hitler postponed the invasion until further notice'. After the victory Churchill broadcast the memorable words to the nation that

never in the history of human conflict was so much owed by so many to so few.

King George VI asked through the churches that Sunday the 8th September be set aside as a Day of Prayer 'for the magnificent victory of our gallant airmen'.

Later in the year there was a national appeal for scrap metal to build aircraft, and the iron railings round many a grave in Ambleside churchyard had to go. London was facing an appalling bombing campaign by the German air force, referred to as the blitz, and the civilian casualties were mounting. 'War work is giving shelter to all refugees and evacuees'.

The first tranche of evacuees from Newcastle arrived in the Ambleside area in 1939. Many were billeted on people unable to manage, and pupils drifted back to Newcastle. It was not until the summer of 1940 that a second serious evacuation of the Dame Allen Girls school complete with all the staff moved from Newcastle to Ambleside. An arrangement was made with the Kelsick school; their pupils attended lessons in the mornings from 8.30 till 1 p.m., and the girls from Dame Allen attended school from 1 p.m. till 5.30. One respondent recalled that the Government gave 7s. 6d., to be collected weekly from the post office, to all households that took in an evacuee. This respondent from the oral history archive said that the evacuees upset the Bed and Breakfast trade because all spare bedrooms were taken up. The B&B trade at that time charged 5/- (25p) per night.

Another respondent recalled

I had a four bed roomed house and a baby at the beginning of the war. I got three evacuees at first and then they said I had room for five! I had two until the end of the war. I used to get 10/- a week for each child, for feeding them, and doing all the washing, and all those white socks . . . I used to make the girls make their own beds . . .

Some girls from Newcastle were very lucky indeed going to one of the big houses. The two that arrived at one of the McIver houses were put in charge of the cook; the household also had a maid, a gardener, a chauffeur and a handyman. The cook subsequently left, and the girls were looked after by the maid who stayed in service throughout the war. The evacuees were definitely kept 'below stairs', but had a good time. This respondent remembers that at school dinners

we ate sheeps' hearts, plenty of potatoes, plenty of vegetables and we had duck eggs! The school dinners cost 4d. but we had very small helpings.

The girls from the Dame Allen school were not the only children to come from Newcastle. This local family took children from the other end of the social scale.

We had four evacuees for five years. I remember them coming to the bus station . . . going on for 11 o'clock at night and all those young children from about 5 or 6 years old up to 14 – there must have been about 30-40 of them got off, gas masks over their shoulders and they looked so lost. I remember them all marching down into the Methodist school room and there they would be distributed out . . . it was late so mother landed home with 16 for that night . . . she put double mattresses on the landings for these children to sleep on.

The two little boys we had were tramps, terrible, they just had what they stood up in and they were filthy dirty and were from a family of about 14.

After the first bombing started the mother of these two brothers wanted them back and the authorities let them go and they weren't away six weeks when they [the authorities] took them off the mother. My mother had kitted them out with good clothes and when they came back they were dressed in rags and covered from head to foot in sores and they had scabies . . . all our toys had to be burnt by the Council . . . the house had to be fumigated . . . you should have seen the lice . . .

The Royal College of Art moved to Ambleside from London and took over the Queens Hotel, and a Church of England orphanage for 80 girls moved from Liverpool to the main McIver house in Ambleside.

Being brought up in an orphanage you haven't really got confidence...you're told what to wear, you wear this, that's your number, your number is on all your clothes, you do this . . . You are not really allowed to think for yourself, you get punished if you disobey. As I said you get a belt across the head if you disobey. We were punished severely . . . shutting people in cupboards things like that. The war was on when I was 14 so I became the second kitchen girl. If you had no family you had to go into service, but I had an auntie in Liverpool . . . My brothers were evacuated to Newlands in the north of the Lake District but we weren't allowed to meet.

When the orphanage first came to Ambleside it arrived with its own teaching staff, so the children had no chance of mixing with the village children. As the war went on the teaching staff were called up, or volunteered for war work, and the governors of the orphanage had no option but to let their charges go to the village school.

Whether because of the evacuees attending the Ambleside school, or because of items currently in the news, in November the vicar wrote:

we have discovered tens and thousands of our children growing up with the scantiest knowledge of what Christianity is or does,

and he went on to put the blame on the Education Act of 1902.

The normal procedure of teaching religion in the Day schools was interfered with by the religious controversies of 40 years ago.

It was not only the advent of the evacuees that changed Ambleside; from 1940 women as well as men were called up and women were given the choice of war work or joining the armed forces. Shorts Sunderland Aircraft had started building flying boats at Troutbeck Bridge, and 'hundreds' came from all over the district to work there.

There was a wonderful canteen and good dinners, and we had socials with dance records, and concerts, and local singers came along. Buses brought people to work . . .

From then on there was not just full employment, but a choice of employment, and Ambleside was never the same again.

At the turn of the year the vicar summed up the past twelve months in the following way.

The year of 1940 saw the capitulation of Belgium, the collapse of France, the miracle of Dunkirk, the terrific air assault which became the Battle of Britain, and the devastation of our cities by indiscriminate night bombing. We cannot be beaten because we refuse to recognise defeat.

In the opinion of the vicar

we are moving towards the climax of the war.

We hear it said that this war is for the preservation of Christianity since the enemy has discarded all moral principle and decencies, and practices any wickedness which may appear to his advantage.

So wrote the vicar in April 1941.

The greatest crime that Hitler and his satellites have committed is their encouragement of evil – they have sought to bring out in ordinary decent people the latent evil, the evil lying dormant . . . the old Adam. We face powers that are of incredible wickedness – this is a Crusade . . .

In June 1941 the vicar wrote about

the unscrupulous and blood-stained Stalin has been deceived and betrayed by the cynical and blood-stained Hitler. We can have no sympathy with Stalin for his pact with Hitler in 1939 was a betrayal of the existing balance of power and enabled the German thug to embark on his career of conquest. And now he is suitably rewarded because Germany invaded Russia. Russia may rise again purified and take on an honoured place in the life of Christian Europe. We wait upon events.

But a month later in July the vicar had modified his approach.

The Russians have fought magnificently with courage and brilliance . . . we shall owe our allies an immense debt. They are taking the shock we were expecting . . .

Later in the year in September the vicar wrote:

we are learning to think differently about the Russians nowadays. This is a war in defence of Christianity.

The thrust of the vicar's argument was that although the Russians were not and could not be considered Christian, it was our duty to give them every support possible.

In 1942 the Allied forces took another blow with the fall of Tobruk.

The loss is a blow due to the defeat of our forces and to the superior generalship of Field-Marshall Rommel. We must give the Devil his due,

wrote the vicar. He then went on to make the pertinent point that

we might have been a bit more prepared for this news if those whose duty it is to issue news and views to us were a little less optimistic and a bit more realistic.

The British Army had to retreat towards Cairo, but later that year, under the generalship of Field-Marshall Bernard Montgomery, the Eighth Army had a resounding victory at El Alamein. The Germans were out gunned, and the battle for North Africa was won. The Allies invaded Italy the following year, and the Germans were for the first time facing retreat on both the Russian front, and on the Italian front.

When Winston Churchill became Prime Minister in 1940 a coalition Government had been formed with the Labour party; the left wing had a strong part to play, together with the trade unionists both within and outside Government, in formulating domestic policies for the future, and one of the main aims was to suggest legislation to help to break down class barriers. Sir William Beveridge, a Liberal planner, had produced a plan for universal social security benefits which pleased the Labour party: the newspapers suggested there would be a New Order after the war, and wrote the vicar, the church would not be exempt from change.

The Government were making plans for Britain after the war even though the end of the war was not in sight. A Ministry of Reconstruction had been formed, and had let it be known that a radical change in the role of the state was envisaged in the future. The plan for universal social security was published by William Beveridge in 1943 which, according to A. J. P. Taylor, had a muted response from the Conservatives. There was talk of a new Ministry of Town Planning. The church magazine outlined the ideas for plans for new houses, some to be constructed in the new garden cities yet to be built.

There were to be blocks of flats which will be almost cities in themselves, and a hundred new towns with their residential, recreational and working quarters all planned.

There was also talk of reforming the monetary system.

By 1942 there was a feeling being expressed locally that society was not only changing, but changing in a radical way. The people who lived in the big houses were cutting back on the costs because they could no longer afford the upkeep. First of all there was the call up of able-bodied men into the armed services; taxes had risen significantly, the cost of wages had risen, and perhaps more to the point, no one now needed to go into domestic service. Because of these factors many of the big houses could no longer be maintained, and throughout the war years there was a steady decline in the occupation of both large houses and estates. Some of the houses were requisitioned for use as schools, and some that remained in occupation did so on a greatly reduced scale.

The magazine included a page on household hints for the housewife, with a theme for every day of the week except Sunday. Monday was for washing hints, Tuesday was for sewing hints, Wednesday for tips on nursing – for instance how to make bandages from white sugar bag linings, Thursday was about economical cooking, Friday had ideas or suggestions for household repairs, and Saturday was devoted to children. In the household section there was advice on how best to use coal dust, how to repair the mangle, and how to repair the kettle when it has been burnt by the fire. Also advice on how to make your own pan scourer, and tips on keeping the flat iron in good condition. As the vicar put it 'ingenuity is the word for these women'.

From 1940 a tight food rationing system was imposed, and as the war went on, more foods were rationed, and the amounts allowed deceased. The wartime rations were approximately 2 oz butter, 3 oz margarine, 1 oz lard, 1 oz cheese, 4 oz meat, 6 oz sugar and one egg per person, per week. But many in both the valleys and the township did not suffer much hardship on account of the rationing. A hotelier said

You see we had our own sheep, our own pigs, our own cattle, your own butter, your own milk, and the jam and things they were very inferior. And the meat ration you got from the butcher well it was so minute you couldn't possibly have managed . . . petrol was rationed, we all had coupons. We ran a hotel in wartime with just one maid . . .

During the war a licence was needed to kill a pig, but as another respondent put it

somehow two pigs always seemed to get killed that day.

With the number of gardens and the tradition of growing both fruit and vegetables even the Liverpool orphanage had fresh vegetables daily. There was food available that was off the ration like rabbits and pheasants, and the Lake Urban District Council made sure the hotels all got extra food rations for the visitors. Throughout the war years annual holidays were taken by civilians whenever possible, and the Lake District was sufficiently remote from the bombing to attract many for their summer break. As was frequently remarked, Ambleside became very busy.

Ambleside entertained oversees troops and airmen who brought their own ration cards with them.

The men had to have done thirty runs on bombing then they would get leave after that, so many days, and they used to come here . . .

The bombing of the big cities continued, and in 1942 the Liverpool College for Girls decided to evacuate to Rydal Hall, and were welcomed by the church in Rydal for both their attendance and choral singing. There was a shortage of clergymen during the war as, of course, those men young enough were working as chaplains to the armed services. The vicar of Ambleside indicated he would like a curate for Rydal, but to add to the difficulties the stipend was only £200 per year.

The call-up has been extended far more widely and deeply than before and we who are left behind have to shoulder very often a double or triple responsibility and often with less resources.

The church expenses still had to be met, and in 1943 they amounted to £408. 12s. 9d., and the offertory money came to £508. 2s. 4d. Kendal Hospital had to be supported, and then there was the Air-Raid Relief Fund, the Red Cross, the Ex-Service Welfare Fund, the King Georges Fund for Sailors, and help was also asked for for Russian Orphans, and so on. This meant there was smaller funding for the various Missionaries.

A Cigarette League had been started to provide cigarettes to the armed forces and following a fête held in the Ambleside Infants' school the magazine was proud to announce that:

The Infants have been greatly pleased to receive two letters from the Middle East thanking them for the cigarettes sent through the Cigarette League with money collected in school on Empire Day. The children had collected 15/- and the League is able to send the cigarettes duty free.

The Prime Minister in one of his famous broadcasts warned of the desperate struggle that lay ahead, and he felt the war was entering difficult days. America had entered the war in 1941 following the bombing of Pearl Harbour by the Japanese, and throughout 1943 tremendous pressure was put on the Allies by Russia to open a second front in Europe. However, Churchill decided we must wait for the right time when we would be fully prepared to invade Europe.

By mid-summer 1944 the plans to invade France were in place and the vicar wrote that when D. Day happened the church would be open all day for prayer. On D. Day itself, 6th June, the King made a broadcast message with a call to prayer. 'Copies of the Kings broadcast will be on the book table . . .'.

Germany is beaten and if they were a normal people they would lay down their arms . . . but we must go on until any thought of Germany making war again under a century will be absurd.
   We can make no sort of bargain with the Nazis.

wrote the vicar in January 1945. This comment followed a battle in the Ardennes which

shows the enemy is still not broken. The history of the human race shows clearly enough that man is better when he is struggling against difficulties. Give him luxury and an easy time and he goes softer and softer till he rots with decay,

and the vicar went on to cite the fall of Rome as an example of what can befall man.

In February the vicar's son was killed while serving in the army 'and it does not help that he was killed in an accident'.

On the 8th May 1945, following Hitler's suicide, the war with Germany ended.

It was right and natural that our rejoicing over the victory should be restrained for we remember the cost and also the fact that there is still a war in the Far East. There should be no attempt to set up a German Government until sometime after the war so that some form of sanity and steadiness be recovered.

The war in Europe ended on the 8th May 1945, and soon after the rejoicing had ceased, the need for new legislation was being discussed in the newspapers. A general election was overdue, and the vicar urged, 'we must take the forthcoming General Election seriously and vote'. In spite of the huge popularity of the Prime Minister Winston Churchill who had led the country to victory, there was a landslide victory for the Labour party. Many, it was said, did not want a return to the conditions of the thirties, and they voted for a radical new approach to the social security system.

The church was facing a crisis nationally because several thousand new priests were needed to fill the vacant posts, and there was also the urgent necessity to get the church schools in order to meet the the new higher standards required by the 1944 Education Act. To add to the difficulties Ambleside parish was told it would have to make a bigger contribution to the costs of the Diocese, and then there was the problem of raising enough money to afford to pay for a curate. At the moment the stipend for the curate stood at £200 per annum, and the parish would have to raise another £100 to attract a deacon or priest. Plans were also made to convert the old parish church of St Anne's into a parish hall which would of course require furnishing . . .

Peace in Europe does not mean perfect tranquillity at home – there are all sorts of strikes; go slows and ferments are popping up like boils on the country's body . . . the chaos caused by the war will take years to clear.

However, in the following month, August 1945, the vicar was happy to report that

at last the nightmare is over. The coming of the atomic bomb is an event loaded with all sorts of possibilities. In the hands of a Hitler it might mean the destruction of civilisation. In the hands of Christians, it – I mean of course the force released by atomic fissure – can be of immense benefit to mankind . . . all men should become really Christian . . . if this does not happen the more dire consequences will fall upon mankind.

Twenty-four men from Ambleside were killed in the second world war, including the vicar's son. According to A. J. P. Taylor about 400,000 Britons were killed in the war: of that number about 300,000 were members of the armed services, and about 100,000 were either civilians or merchant seamen.

By 1946 the War Memorial Appeal collected a total of £277. 6s. 4d. 'which is sufficient to put names on a decorated tablet in the church'.

The conversion of Britain had long been the aim of the evangelists, and it is interesting to note that in the summer of 1945 a report was written by the Committee of the Church Assembly on the theme of conversion. The report recognised and tried to account for the growing indifference that many people were beginning to show towards organised religion. Congregations were beginning to get smaller. The vicar of Ambleside wanted a greater commitment from the parishioners, and said he expected 'all ages' to attend Sunday school once on a Sunday. 'You must think of duty as well as of rights'. In the spring of 1946 the vicar organised a Missionary Sunday to try to get recruits into the service.

A lecture was given in Ambleside on the newly formed United Nations organisation which started in San Fransisco before moving to its permanent home in New York. The underlying ideal was to pick up and develop where the League of Nations left off, and the theme the lecturer wanted to convey was that only by the United Nations holding together could anyone have any future at all. At the end of the meeting seventy local people gave their names as willing to join a United Nations Association, and a branch was duly formed.

The words of the Prime Minister, Clement Atlee were quoted in the magazine.

The greatest task that faces us today is to bring home to all people before it is too late that our civilisation can only survive by the acceptance and practice in international relations and in our national life of the Christian principle that we are members of one another.

The war might be over but food rationing became more severe as the shortages worsened, and in 1946 bread became rationed. Food shortage was bad in Britain, but there was famine in both Europe and India. There were shortages of goods of all kinds in the shops, and there were shortages of people in a variety of professions. A plea went out for girls to take up nursing as a career, and in order to fill the vacancies a concession was made to girls who had already completed two years work in fever hospitals: the concession was that in future the fever hospital experience would qualify them to undertake the state registered course. The starting salary for a nursing recruit was £90 per annum, rising to £120 on qualification.

Meanwhile the Royal College of Art which had been evacuated to Ambleside during the war was returning to London, but not before they had painted a large mural of the rushbearing ceremony inside the church. After the war G. G. Ransome A.R.C.A painted a huge mural of the rushbearing ceremony, and when the painting was completed it was dedicated by the Bishop of Carlisle.

The painting will serve as a memento of the presence of the Royal College of Art in Ambleside during the years of war.

The Liverpool College for Girls who had been evacuated to Rydal Hall were returning to Huyton. The girls would be sadly missed by Rydal church as they provided both choir, and a large proportion of the congregation. Rydal church meanwhile was unable to give communion as there was no vicar available to help out.

The Social Reforms

There had been some opinions expressed as long ago as 1909 in the Minority Report of the Poor Law Commission which reported that year – the work largely of Sydney and Beatrice Webb, leading members of the early socialist Fabian Society, – which discussed a non-contributory system of public maintenance for the unemployed, but neither Parliament nor public opinion was ready for such a radical proposition. This was because society at that time still liked to make judgments on the deserving and undeserving poor. It was not until the mass unemployment of the interwar years that these concepts were considered flawed, and it was these non-judgmental ideas that were seminal to the Beveridge report in 1943.

The Labour Government that swept to power in the election of July 1945 was determined that among other measures poverty and destitution would become a thing of the past. From then on benefits were paid to claimants who had no other means of support, regardless of whether they were deserving or otherwise, and a 'safety-net' was created for those who were for what ever reason ineligible to claim insurance benefits. The Government's intention was to plan for full employment, and legislation was passed for universal unemployment benefit to be paid to people through the national insurance scheme, should they be out of work between jobs. A National Health Service, free to everyone, was passed into law, and initially the service included free dentistry and glasses.

The Poor Law was abolished by the National Assistance Act of 1948; the workhouses then finally ceased to exist – though many were converted into long stay wards for the elderly infirm. In fact since the mass unemployment of the 1930s the workhouses had not been taking in families, and were used in the main by tramps, the homeless, and for the elderly. One respondent from the oral history archive recalled visiting the Ulverston workhouse just before the war, when she found:-

> *if a couple went in they were separated – women to one end, the women's wing, and the men to the other end – the men's wing, it was dreadful.*

Some of the older workhouses had a wing used for what used to be referred to as the 'pauper lunatics'; these wings were frequently converted to psychiatric units under the new national health service.

A Childrens Act was passed in 1948 to stop child abuse, and a special childrens department to be run by the local authorities was created. But the vicar expressed some doubts about the new radicalism.

> *Forty years ago there was a large class of people who were compelled by force of circumstances to live in poverty, and sometimes in distress. Today it is almost right to say that there are no poor people . . . or perhaps it would be truer to say that a new class is becoming the 'poor' – those who are, in these days of high prices and taxation, forced to live on small fixed incomes with no hope of increase or of bonus.*

When the programme of the present Government is carried out fully we shall find ourselves in a strange world where the old securities are gone . . . this will have a great effect on the church and on all voluntary societies and will make their work much more difficult.

The church magazine

There are two urgent problems that face the Church Assembly – (1) The need for more clergy and (2) the grave financial situation caused by the increasing prices of goods and labour affecting most clergy whose incomes are fixed at a low level . . . the whole situation now facing the church is one of great complexity.

To illustrate the problem the church was facing nationally the vicar wrote that the:

Diocese of Southwark had only 50 undamaged churches out of a total of 450 which existed before the war. During the bombing of London many churches were totally destroyed, as were vicarages, church halls and church schools. The church faced a shortage of manpower and needed another 5,000 men to train for the ministry; the training lasted four years, and cost £1,000 to train each man.

There was also a loss from mining royalties with the nationalisation of coal,

which will cost the church £150,000 per annum, and the Tithe Act will deprive the church of a further £350,000 per annum.

At Christmas the vicar was uncertain of the future.

We are still suffering from the war-time shortages and difficulties . . . added to all that inevitable unease, the Government are pressing forward with a large programme of social reform and . . . we will need our war-time steadiness and readiness to make sacrifices.

In 1947, 57 people came forward for confirmation which was an increase on the previous year. The church had 16 sidemen, a choir, a choirmaster and an organist, and a verger who doubled as a sexton and was paid £4. 10s. per week.

The economic conditions remained depressing to the vicar, but not on grounds of unemployment.

We must cleanse our public life of the awful blots that disfigure it – impurity, intemperance, dishonesty and sloth.

In 1947 the Denning Report on divorce reform was published and the vicar was against any change.

In 1855 there were fewer than 20 divorces in the whole of the United Kingdom. In 1946 there were 46,000 cases awaiting the courts. The root cause of the monumental increase in divorce cases lies in the widespread if uninformed opinion that the idea of the permanence of marriage may be regarded as a fad of religious people, and that the state will encourage and assist the termination of the contract where reasonable grounds for doing so can be shown . . .

The following month he went on to ask

Is England a Christian country or must it now be considered heathen? In 1946, 300,000 towels were stolen from the Great Western Railway; receipts at the grey hound totaliser came to £137,715,273; £530,000,000 was spent on alcohol, and £680,000,000 was spent on tobacco. Of the entrants to the Royal Navy only 23% knew the Lords Prayer. This is a fall from the Christian standards . . . we must have a Day of Prayer.

In November the wedding of Princess Elizabeth to Prince Philip was celebrated in Westminster Abbey; this gave both the vicar and the congregation something to cheer about.

After considerable discussion it was agreed that the memorial to the fallen in the second world war should be placed inside the church and not on the plinth dedicated to those that lost their lives in the first world war.

The Dedication of the tablet to the dead in the war 1939-1945 will be on 9th December 1947.

The local church was fortunate to appoint a curate to work at Rydal, but he has 'no house or means of buying one'. The other problem was the salary which 'must be increased to £320 per annum and we shall have to open a subscription list'. The curate duly started and restarted evensong.

'The congregations are too small and there is a deterioration of religious faith'. The vicar felt he had said all he could say to the people of Ambleside, and it was time for him to leave after 15 years in the post. He obtained another living in Grange.

A refugee from the war, the artist Kurt Schwitters, who had lived in Ambleside for three years, died in January 1948.

President Truman of the United States made a speech which was commented on in the magazine. Mr Truman gave a warning

in which he gave democracy five years breathing space to arm itself for the atomic war of 1953 . . . and the warning was based on factual information.

The vicar wrote

there are no depths to which unregenerate mankind will not sink in the achievement of its purpose. Atomic weapons may destroy your bodies but only one thing can destroy your souls: unrepented sin.

The thrust of the article was we must not lament the passing of western civilisation so much, but we must save our souls.

The reason for the despair was the 'iron curtain', a term aptly coined by Winston Churchill, which Russia had cast across Eastern Europe. In his memoirs 'The Gathering Storm', quoted in the magazine, Churchill had written

Looking back over the period stretching from the Armistice to the outbreak of the second world war we are appalled at the story of folly, stupidity and shortsightedness which

characterised so many of those in positions of responsibility in all the nations. Compromise and expediency are of little value.

The new vicar, Archdeacon Wilkinson was inaugurated,

There are two powers that contend for the soul of man – Christianity and atheistic materialism expressed now in communism. The battle is joined. The fight is on.

This was not the only battle on his hands; the new vicar clearly – and rightly – also identified apathy as the enemy that had to be fought, and he was critical of the 'low morality and low standards of behaviour' he saw around him. 'We have lost the habit of worship'. The congregation was leaching away. The magazine took on a didactic tone, and the vicar's monthly letter began to read like a sermon.

The vicar was active in the parish and tried hard to reestablish the position of the church in the community. He started a young wives' group which gathered momentum over the next few years, he encouraged the mothers' union, a church youth club opened, and he started a special service for men.

The big event for 1950 was the commemoration the centenary of Wordsworth's death on the 23rd of April. The Bishop of Carlisle spoke at morning service at Rydal, and in the evening the preacher was the Reverend Christopher Wordsworth, a direct descendant of the poet. After evensong there was poetry readings at Rydal Mount, the home of the poet, until late into the evening. Special music had been written, and the vicar was anxious that

local people must take part in this memorable centenary, please obtain your programme well in advance . . .

Financial problems beset the church; the Waifs and Strays Society which had been renamed the Church of England Childrens Society, had run up a deficit of £60,000, and consequently the little home of St Anne's had to be sold and the children moved elsewhere. The church steeple was in need of expensive repair costing £5,000, and there were the expenses of making improvements to the vicarage, and to the schools, and a house had to be found for the curate.

The church was hampered both by lack of manpower, and by lack of funds: but in spite of what the vicar referred to as 'unmistakable signs of spiritual malnutrition', there is no doubt that the church tried hard to rally the congregation and provide the social life of the township.

In 1951 Mr Wilkinson was promoted to Liverpool Cathedral and a new vicar, the Archdeacon of Westmorland and Hon Canon of Carlisle Cathedral, the Reverend S. C. Bulley was appointed take up the vacancy in Ambleside. Again the new vicar wanted to regenerate the people starting with vigorous Sunday schools; the present ones were 'very much below average size and there was an absence of young people in the general congregation'.

As an example of evangelical zeal on Christmas Day, Mr Bulley had communion services at 6 a.m., 7 a.m. and 8 a.m., Matins was held at 10.45, another communion service followed at 12 noon, and the day ended with evensong at 4 p.m. On December 26th there was a communion service at 10 a.m., with evensong at 6 p.m., and the same services were held on both December 27th and December 28th. There was no lack of enthusiasm.

In January 1952 there were

grave words from our Prime Minister Mr Winston Churchill about our economic position.

There were also

wars in Korea and Malaya, and frustration which seem to meet every promise of some understanding between the two power blocks in which insincerity and lying propaganda have driven the United Nations . . . we are in the midst of a crisis now.

The solution was to go

back to evangelism and education – those twin agencies of hope to which the church must inevitably dedicate its resources of money and man power this century.

On February 1952 King George VI died; the church tolled the tenor bell.

It is not just the King is dead . . . it was our King, the man who on Christmas Day had spoken to us from his fireside as we sat around ours . . .

More than 900 people crowded into Ambleside church at 7 p.m. on the day of the Kings Funeral and joined in the official order of service issued by Her Majesty's command.

King George was a man with deep faith in God and His purpose. Sunday by Sunday he attended public worship along with his family; he called his people to prayer; he prayed himself.

The vicar thought it was time for him to voice his opinion on the 'experiment known as the Welfare State'.

Broadly speaking it is an experiment to achieve equality without foregoing liberty. It aims to build a social democracy with all its economic implications without sacrificing our traditions, without the loss of individual freedom or the undermining of responsibility. However, there is something gravely wrong . . . the religious basis of the conception is being overlooked.

Although the Band of Hope had been forgotten if not disbanded, the problem of alcoholism remained a worry.

Convictions for drunkenness in the United Kingdom in 1946 was 20,545, but by 1951 this number had risen to 51,239.

If conditions in the refugee camps were disheartening it was not as bad, wrote the vicar, as life for the

millions held behind the iron curtain who lived a life of miserable degrading servitude.

There were still

millions of refugees in the world. In Germany alone there are nearly 10,000,000 refugees of whom something approaching 8,000,000 have been expelled from other European countries and about 2,000,000 have fled Communist oppression in East Germany. Clothing, which has first been washed and repaired, should be left in the church and will be sent off in sacks.

The destructive power of secular materialism is invading every area of human activity,

wrote the vicar.

The decline in the sanctions of religion in everyday life is responsible for the serious increase in crime. There are now twice as many indictable offences in a single year than before the war and we now have two and a half times as many in prison . . .

From the tone of the magazine one might expect the congregation to be falling, but in fact numbers rose from 1948, when at the Easter count there were 298 attenders, to 423 in 1953, slightly down on the year before. Another statistic to show that the church still held a significant place in society was that nearly 12,000 people signed the visitors book in 1953. The financial needs of the church dominated the magazine, with the stark fact that to maintain itself the church in 1953 needed £1,670 and had only '£430 as secure guaranteed endowment'. The vicarage was another problem. Built in the exuberant days of the early 1880s it had '19 rooms and 49 doors': the vicars stipend, with the Easter offering, came to £589. 19s. 9d. in 1952. This compares with the starting salary of a Public Health Inspector which in 1956 was advertised as commencing at £670. 7s. 0d. p.a.

The Coronation of Queen Elizabeth took place on 2nd June 1953, and the church held a night vigil service on Coronation eve, followed by a communion service at 7.30 a.m. and again at 9.30. 'The congregation could then return home to listen to the broadcast from Westminster Abbey on their wireless sets', wrote the vicar. But television reception had come to Ambleside by 1952, and doubtless many more took advantage of the new technology and watched the proceedings on their black and white television sets.

Later in the year the advent of commercial television raised important questions about responsibilities of Government and the role of the B.B.C. There were many weighty letters in 'The Times', according to the vicar, under headings like 'Let Well Alone', and 'Playing with Fire'. The churches condemned the very idea of introducing commercial television, and the vicar said the all Christians had a special duty to perform to make their views known through their church councils.

Local Education

Little or no extra money was available during the war to be spent on school buildings, and with the number of evacuees the pupil numbers increased in all the local schools. A respondent who was a Headmistress in a church school in Windermere in 1940 mentioned some of the problems.

> *There were the outside toilets. There were no doors on them, they just had a sacking curtain for privacy. Some classes we had over 50 pupils in . . . we had school dinners then, but in another school and we all kind of traipsed along every dinner time and back again.*
>
> *Oh many a time I have coped with those wretched rats . . . I sent for the rodent man . . . he said now they'll probably have come from the churchyard . . . then he told me they were probably under the floor of the big hall . . . I once saw this wretched rat in the corner of the playground . . .*

Education reform had been promised since the end of the first world war, and in 1943 a new Bill was published. Rather surprisingly the vicar had this to say about it. He thought the Bill

> *will probably mean the loss of many schools to the Church of England, but the gain for the children of the Country as a whole is so great the church is willing to loose schools rather than resist the Bill.*

The essence of the Bill was the promise of secondary education for all children. This would entail raising the school leaving age to fifteen from fourteen, and it was the considered view of the educationalists that all children would benefit. The Education Bill introduced the idea that at the age of eleven children would go to a school most suited to their scholastic potential, and therefore there would be three kinds of secondary schools to select from. The academic child would go to a grammar school, the child interested in the applied sciences would go to a technical school, and the largest group would go to what was named a 'modern' school. The 'eleven plus' examination system was about to be introduced.

Although the vicar had welcomed the Education Act of 1944 on the grounds that all children should have secondary education, when the County Council published the plans the vicar was far from certain he could agree. The primary ground for rejection of the plans was that Ambleside – or the church – would loose control of children over the age of eleven, because Ambleside would cease to be an educational centre.

> *Some of the County Councils in making plans for the transition seem to be affected by megalomania and picture huge schools housing children by the thousands.*

The vicar rejected the plans to build a central school on grounds of expense, and on grounds that travel for all 11 year olds would 'entail hardship for delicate children, with wet clothing in the winter weather'. Many children attending the Ambleside schools walked up to three or four miles to school daily, and there are many stories in the oral history tapes to illustrate how the teachers struggled to dry out wet clothing before the return journey through rain or snow. This was a problem which had always existed for children attending the local primary schools. He also argued that the reason the Council wanted to build large schools was for ease of administration, and the needs of the individual child and the development of his personality would be overlooked.

What was proposed for Ambleside initially was a conversion of the boys' school into a senior school for both boys and girls, and the girls' junior school would serve all children under eleven. The Kelsick Grammar school would be enlarged from the current size of 135 pupils to an intake of 250 pupils who would be selected by examination at the age of 11. Children attending the all-age or 'modern' school would stay on till the age of 15, and a new class room was built to accommodate the extra year. Although the school-leaving age was raised to 15 there was little enthusiasm expressed. At first children could leave school on their 15th birthday, then regulations stipulated they could leave school at the end of the term they were 15, and then they were told they had to stay till the end of the school year.

In October the Westmorland County Council Development Plan for schools was published and the vicar was outraged.

This plan will mean considerable changes. The Kelsick Grammar will cease to exist. Two new schools will be erected somewhere between Ambleside and Windermere for all children of both areas . . . the public must be ready to throw its weight into the scales at the proper moment . . . the fight is on . . .

In 1948 Archdeacon Wilkinson took over the crusade to keep the church control of the school. He wrote:

following the 1944 Education Act the state is now prepared to put up 50% of capital costs for new church schools, and it will be a great loss to the community if they cease to be church schools. However, the church nationally . . . in view of financial stringency . . . is no longer given large bequests of money . . . and is not always able to match the necessary funding.

The Catholics are very active and alive to the situation and that church is not letting its schools go! Unless we bestir ourselves there will be a majority of places where the only schools are County and Roman Catholic!

On January 1st 1950 the vicar made a passionate plea

for the retention of church schools. Admittedly the Council Schools have Religious Instruction but we feel there is a great gain if it can be supplemented by church syllabuses with a definite point of view. The church maintains teacher training colleges where teachers who are convinced churchmen can train in church schools. We must maintain our schools because they are a feature of English education which has contributed so much . . .

In April 1950 the magazine printed a personal appeal by the Bishop of Carlisle. The Bishop said there was now a financial crisis because the Education Act had laid down a higher standard for the buildings and equipment, as well as for the educational attainments of the children.

The diocese is determined to keep some of the church schools . . . but it is highly improbable we can keep them all but we want to make a fight for those which by real effort can be retained as full church schools.

The Bishop was unable to confirm if Ambleside school would continue as a church school. Ambleside had promised to raise £250 from the parents and congregation, but in the event had only raised £206. 2s. 1d. The church council had to make up the difference from the free will offerings.

Under the 1944 Education every Local Education Authority had to survey all the schools in their area. This inspection included all church schools as well as the Council schools, and the idea was to bring them all up to the same standard. The church schools in Ambleside presented many problems and it was twelve years after the passing of the Act that the necessary improvements were completed. Finally the schools received a favourable report and the

most recent improvements being the installation of up-to-date sanitary and cloakroom accommodation in the Junior school and of electric light in the Infants' school.

The 1959 Ambleside school inspection was satisfactory and

the Infants' school had been brought up to the standard of the Ministry of Education Building Regulations . . . save for deficiencies of a dozen square feet in some classrooms.

In the same year the Kelsick Grammar school won two state scholarships to Oxbridge –

Kelsick school is the smallest grammar school in the county . . . this achievement torpedoes pretty effectively many of the arguments of those who think that everything, schools in particular, must be bigger to be better.

In 1957 there was great indignation expressed in the magazine because Westmorland Education Committee proposed to stop maintaining Kelsick Grammar school.

Their purpose is to build what is called a Comprehensive School which would provide for secondary education for all the 11+ children from a wide area.

The church was pleased to note that the Lake District Urban Council was against the plans. The Kelsick school had 170 pupils, and the vicar was Chairman of the Governors. The vicar was not reassured that there will be a grammar school stream in the new purpose-built school.

The Comprehensive school experiment has not caught on! All associations of secondary school teachers have spoken against it! It would be a sad day for England if ever the church contracts out of the field of education in which she was the pioneer . . .

The vicar quoted Archbishop William Temple who said of the system of the church/state partnership

its primary purpose is its duality. The Archbishop looked with horror on the possibility of a grey uniform system of education in which the state was all-powerful, controlling even the training colleges.

'The first comprehensive school in the whole country was Windermere Grammar School in 1946'.

This bold assertion was made by a respondent from the Oral History archive who became the first Headmaster of the Lakes School:

Before the war Windermere Grammar School had about 80 to 100 pupils. Then the war came and Dame Allens School from Newcastle was evacuated and they became part of the grammar school and they had to provide more classrooms. After the war Windermere G.S. became 'bilateral'; we took in all boys and divided them in half and gave what we thought a grammar education with French to half the boys, and the other half had a secondary modern education. The technical schools rarely got off the ground because they were too expensive.

There were four main schools in the district in 1958; the Windermere Grammar school which took all the boys from Windermere unless they went elsewhere. The Old College secondary modern school for girls was a one form entry for Windermere girls, and then there was the one stream entry to the Kelsick Grammar school in Ambleside which was largely taken up by girls. And last but not least there were the children over the age of 11 attending the Ambleside all age school.

The decision to build a comprehensive school was passed by the casting vote of the Chairman of Westmorland County Council!

The vicar wrote in the magazine:

In January 1961 the news came through that the Ministry of Education had decided to approve the building of a new bilateral school at Calgarth which will involve the disappearance of Kelsick and Windermere grammar schools, and the Old College school . . . the fight to preserve Kelsick has been waged . . . we can only regret . . . and offer sympathy.

Westmorland County started building the Lakes School in 1963 and it opened in 1965 as an amalgamation of the four schools with 570 pupils which, by 1977, had grown to 998.

Changes were also happening at the Charlotte Mason College and the Fairfield school. Ever since Miss Mason started her teacher training college she ran the Fairfield School school for about 30 pupils of mixed ages, and the school existed primarily for students to practice on.

It is the intention that the college should be taken over by the state, and because that will mean an increase in the number of students there, a decrease in the number of girls at Fairfield is inevitable in order to provide accommodation. The college will be state-controlled, but the school, while independent will not provide, as at present education for older girls.

The Fairfield school which never had many children over the age of eleven on the register, closed in the early 1962.

The Fairfield school girls, though day pupils, were expected to attend Matins every Sunday and the vicar commented that the changes proposed for the management of Charlotte Mason College from a P.N.E.U. teaching establishment to Westmorland County Teacher Training College 'inevitably weakened the ties that once bound it so closely to the church'.

The Charlotte Mason College had started a three-year teacher training course in 1949 and was one of the first independent colleges to inaugurate such a scheme.

The Charlotte Mason College had appealed unsuccessfully for recognition by the Ministry of Education in the 1930s, but on their third attempt when they had revamped their methods they were awarded recognition in 1950. Miss Mason was a fiercely independent-minded person who wanted her college to remain likewise. Given the fact that her Christianity was at the core of her being, it is strange that she did not want the college to be taken over by the church who owned and ran a considerable number of teacher training colleges. Up until the time the college was taken over by Westmorland Education Committee the students at the college attended Matins or Evensong as they always had done, and during term time there would be at least eighty young women in the congregation. It was said by an oral history respondent that many of the students were the daughters of the clergy.

In the 1920s the 'King's School' moved to premises in Ambleside; it was a minor public school, offering secondary education to boys, but by the late 1950s had run into financial difficulties and had to close. The school supported the Church of England, and boys had to attend matins. Within a decade St Mary's church lost the support of two private schools, and the College attenders dwindled with the change to state ownership.

Lakes Urban District Council

At the outbreak of war the Council decided to have a lecture on

How to salvage for human consumption food that has been exposed to the action of poison gas and how to insure the destruction of contaminated food.

The importance of fuel economy, and food economy, and the question of food rationing for the hotels were discussed, along with the question of whether gardeners in private employment should be released from the call up. But the main question was about the provision of air raid shelters which in the end did not have priority. Identity cards were issued to all citizens, and a rota of voluntary fire watchers established. Ambleside wanted an air raid siren; the response from Westmorland County Council was they agreed 'they would provide 30% of the costs but the remaining 70% would have to come by public subscription'. Ambleside agreed to these proposals and duly organised a public subscription list. Needless to say all major building works were put on hold.

The first year of the war was given the name 'phoney' because little happened. However, by 1940 war was truly engaged with the occupation of a large part of Europe by Germany, and from then on there were frequent bombing raids on London and the major cities. There were three waves of evacuees to the Lake District largely because the area seemed far enough away from London. In total 891 evacuees were billeted locally; included in this number were whole schools that took over hotels and large houses. In July 1944 there was the third wave of evacuees because of the menace of the flying bombs over London and the south east. It was the job of the Council to place the evacuees in suitable homes with the help of a billeting officer.

In 1944 an anomaly presented by the Lords Day Observance Society was discussed in the Council. The current situation was much the same as it had been since the mid-Victorian era when the Lords Day Observance Society could and did prevent Sunday entertainment, and it was considered that this position no longer expressed the opinion of the great majority of the people. The armed services wanted a relaxation of the rules, for example they wanted the cinemas to be allowed to open on Sundays, but it was up to Parliament to introduce the necessary legislation. The Council voted that they could see no objection to a relaxation of the rules and they urged Parliament to act. This duly happened and from then on and very gradually Sunday ceased to be a day apart.

The Council agreed with the Government, following the principles laid down in a White Paper, that after the war the national policy would be to achieve full employment, and that lessons must be learned from the aftermath of the first world war. The Council endorsed the principle that there must be a big drive for new decent houses, and 'powers were given to the council to requisition unoccupied houses for the inadequately housed'. In 1946 a National Housing Conference was convened.

Although the County Council controlled education finance, the Lakes Urban District Council was concerned that any reconstruction should take place on existing sites. The Council agreed with the church authorities that broadly speaking, even though there was a legal requirement under the new Act of 1944 for the authorities to provide secondary education for all, in fact little change was necessary except extra classroom provision for the 14 year olds to stay in school until they were 15.

When the new Labour government came to power in 1945, their huge legislative programme included measures that to a limited extent diminished the powers of the local Councils. In July 1946 the gas companies were nationalised; the council was unhappy about the proposals but agreed to cooperated with the new Ministry of Fuel and Power. Electricity was nationalised later in the Parliamentary session in 1947. Before that the Windermere and District Electricity Supply Co Ltd were asked by the Council *if they were considering the question of extending the area of supply to the villages of Chapel Stile and Elterwater, Hartsop and Deepdale.*

The Electricity company said it was indeed their aim to supply more customers, and they planned

extensive works with the object of affording consumers a cheaper and more abundant supply of electricity.

Nationalisation followed and the newly formed North West Electricity Board considered supplying electricity to the valleys but had to confront the planners and the Friends of the Lake District. The problem or dilemma that caused the delay until 1956, was the fact that underground cables were expensive, and overhead pylons were unacceptably ugly. Eventually a compromise was reached, and power lines were supplied to the relief to all villagers.

The need for an automatic telephone exchange and for telephone kiosks to be put in the valleys

was also minuted.

The Lake District National Park was created in 1946, and became the planning authority instead of Westmorland and Cumberland County Councils. The concept of creating a series of National Parks had been discussed before the war and was based on the idea that because Britain was a highly industrialised heavily populated island, people needed access to natural unspoilt countryside. The Lake District, as one respondent put it,

had a head start because of the National Trust, a charity set up in the Lake District in 1895 by Act of Parliament, and the National Trust was the largest landowner in the Park.

As a result planning controls became more complex and stringent, and the bureaucracy increased again when the Town and Country Planning Act was passed in 1947.

Gifts of food were sent to the Lake District from South Africa and Australia and 'it was the duty of the council to distribute the food parcels to the local residents'. Although the war had ended in 1945 there was no let up in hardship in the district. Food remained rationed and if anything the ration was reduced, clothing was rationed, and all goods were in short supply.

The water supply to the Langdale valleys was always unsatisfactory and after much discussion, and intervention from the Medical Officer of Health, a water main was laid to Chapel Stile in 1949. New houses were being built by the Council, and slowly the houses unfit for human habitation was closed down, but central Government did not consider the Council was doing enough. Early in 1952 a letter was received from the Ministry of Housing and Local Government

to request the Council to do all they can to expedite the completion of the houses now under construction and in addition to make necessary plans for an expanding programme over the next three years.

On the 8th February 1952 the Councillors minuted:

Whereas it has pleased almighty God to call to his mercy our late Sovereign Lord King George 6th of blessed and Glorious memory by whose decease the crown is solely and rightfully come to the high and mighty Princess Elizabeth Alexandra Mary we therefore the Lords Spiritual and Temporal . . . proclaim she becomes Queen of this realm and all her other Realms and Territories . . .

This proclamation was read at the Market Cross in Ambleside, and

a large number of inhabitants were present on the occasion together with children attending the schools in the town.

A year later on the 9th March 1953 the death of Queen Mary was announced; the Council sent the Queen an address of condolence. The old Queen did not live long enough to see her granddaughter crowned in Westminster Abbey two months later.

In 1956 the Council decided the time had come to stop recording the minutes in copperplate hand writing as they had done since the inception of local government some sixty years earlier. However, some of the issues that concerned the Council at the end of the nineteenth century still pertained. Petitions to clean up the streams were still being received and the 'names of 300 persons called for the permanent prevention of pollution of the Fishbeck'. But the 'stinking holes' were gone forever; Council house building went on at a good pace, and extended to the villages; slum clearance, which the Council said in 1955 would take ten years, was achieved in the 1960s. The sanitary inspectors were concerned that the remaining privies or earth closets that were still in use were converted to water closets, and they pursued the owners to comply.

It will be recalled that in the first issue of the church magazine in 1879, the vicar had urged the parishioners to be on their guard over the Whitsun holiday. Over the span of the years there would appear to be little change in the behaviour of the young because in 1962

provision was made for extra police supervision in the Ambleside/Grasmere area over the Whitsun bank holiday.

It was later recorded that there was an

increasing problem with hooliganism, and the Senior warden was requested to consult with the voluntary wardens on possible remedies regarding litter and the damage to property.

The senior warden recorded

there were all sorts of horrendous messes all over the place . . . I was clearing with volunteer help litter that had accumulated perhaps over a couple of decades . . .

During the post-war years the local councils produced guide books, the Lake District National Park advertised widely, and to promote the area further a festival was organised in 1964. Tourism created wealth, and the region prospered as never before. The earlier concerns about traffic, and obstruction caused first by carriages then cars, had continued to exercise both the Councillors and the police ever since council records started. With the coming of the motorways in the 1960s, and an ever increasing number of cars and coaches on the roads, the Lake District was no longer inaccessible. The big houses were split into flats, or turned into guest houses or nursing homes. Cottages that came on the market were quickly bought up as second homes; in some villages and hamlets it was said almost half the houses became second homes or holiday accommodation, and a considerable number of wealthy middle class people retired to the district. Ambleside became 'gentrified'.

In 1966 the Council sent a

formal objection to British Rail because of the new practice of passengers having to change at Oxenholme for the London train, instead of the Windermere coaches being coupled to the train as previously.

This practice had not altered since the train service first came to Windermere in 1847.

The Church Magazine

1954 opened with a gloomy message from the vicar:

over the world hangs the black cloud of Marxist Communism with its avowed aim of world domination. Millions have never been released from tyranny and many who were released from Nazism have now been crushed.

However, by June the church was able to celebrate its centenary, and as a Guest of Honour they were delighted to welcome the Reverend Lionel Fell, grandson of the Reverend Irton Fell who was the first incumbent when the church was built. The celebration included an Open Day for the schools, a parish outing to Morecambe, and a special booklet was written entitled 'From Strength to Strength', costing 1/6d a copy, and it was 'issued to every household'. At the end of the centenary celebrations the church bells were rung to tell the people of Ambleside that the target of £5,000 towards repairs to the fabric of the church had been reached.

The international conflicts continued to give concern:

Christian people everywhere must be sorely concerned about the trend of things in South Africa where the South African Government is seeking to make the Europeans, who represent only one sixth of the population, permanently dominant. This hateful 'apartheid' policy must inevitably lead to tension and strife . . . these festering sores within our own Commonwealth . . . non Europeans will never have the same political rights as Europeans rights . . . there will never be social equality.

The vicar then quoted the words of St Paul 'Christ is all in all'.

The words of Lord Justice Denning, Master of the Rolls, were music to the church, and quoted in the magazine.

Public Opinion should condemn adultery . . . it is not the concern of the parties alone but of the whole community because it struck at the foundation of marriage. It is no bar to advancement in any of the offices of state whereas any other form of stealing would mean the end of a career.

There was no doubt that standards were changing, more marriages were breaking down, but the church firmly resisted any challenge to their conviction that marriage was a commitment for life.

The conflict of the day is between the religious and the secular humanist. If you throw away religion you are left without any absolute moral authority to govern individual and social conduct. Morality becomes relative . . .

The absolutist position of teetotalism had been declining in church of England circles for some years, and it is interesting to note a shift in the moral position away from total abstention. The Bishop of London opened a Church of England Temperance Society out-patients clinic, and said

Addiction to alcohol may be at the beginning a sin, or even a crime, but before very long it becomes a disease not only of the mind but of the body. But thank God it is curable.

The magazine during the mid-1950s continued to report increased congregations, and increase in the electoral role, and an increase in the offertory money. The magazine published the following statistics:

75% of all children in the town attend Sunday school. Of the other 25% only the tiniest minority are Methodists or Catholics.

The vicar goes on

90% of all Ambleside children are baptised in the Church of England . . . therefore there are about 10% of children who are wandering and should be shepherded . . .

Ambleside was fortunate in finding a curate willing to come and help; but this appointment meant more money was needed to cover church expenses. The vicar made the comment that

although Ambleside was a place of considerable wealth during the first hundred years of the church, the church had received no substantial legacies for endowment purposes.

He wrote:

The growth of the welfare state with the nationalisation of hospitals, towards whose provision pious people contributed so richly in legacies in time past, has had the effect of narrowing the field for the exercise of charitable impulse. Vast sums used to be left to the hospitals. There is now no need for such legacies and this should encourage church people . . .

The vicar was obviously torn between urging the congregation to give support the more traditional charities, and yet he was concerned with the aftermath of the war.

In 1956 there were still 70,000 people in the refugee camps in Germany, Austria, Greece and Italy, and of these 15,000 are children and another 15,000 are old and ill.

There was a United Nations Refugee week when

the flags of all member states of the United Nations waved gaily in the breeze at Charlotte Mason College.

However, soon after this event the Russians invaded Hungary,

The massacre of Hungary illustrated the creed of Marxist Communism with its perfidy, intrigue, and bestial behaviour that makes mens hearts bleed for the Hungarians . . .

The hope of Communism has proved wholly illusory . . . the creed which promised to eradicate evil at a single sweep ends in a reign of injustice, terror and murder. Christianity and Marxism are fundamentally opposed. What can we do? The United Nations have passed resolution after resolution . . . The United Nations is not equipped to do anything . . . it is like stopping Niagara Falls with a tooth brush . . .

Agencies like the World Health Organisation, or United Nations Education, Scientific and Cultural Organisation, or United Nations Refugee Fund have made a great contribution – but if only the Christian church had been more vigorous against the evils of the world like hunger, illiteracy and poverty.

The Ambleside church did what it had always done and appealed for clothing that would be parcelled and sent to Hungary.

A prominent Methodist Minister preached at St Mary's and his message was that

there is no clear religious revival among us yet . . . no obvious awakening among the masses of artisan workers . . . but the intellectuals no longer regard Christianity as beneath contempt.

At Easter in 1957 the church had 550 communicants with a high percentage of young people and it was the biggest congregation many could remember. The Gallop Poll in a National newspaper suggested 28% attended church whereas a few years before only 10% attended.

The vicar commented on the need for a public library in Ambleside as the need was met only to a very limited extent by the Armitt library. He also wanted a public swimming pool to be built to meet the needs of '700 children in schools in and around Ambleside'. Reading books was to be applauded, but the vicar had strong words about the vogue for comics.

The practice of cremation had gained in popularity since the end of the second world war, but the church was decidedly against the practice of scattering ashes 'over the fells I love'. The vicar went on to describe the practice as 'maudlin, indecent and unhygienic. Ashes should be buried'.

People are better off than they have ever been before. The money is going on motor cars, television sets, radiograms, dry shavers, washing machines, electric irons and expensive toys. More cigarettes than ever are being smoked despite the warnings about lung cancer. People are eating less bread, but more fruit, fish and meat. More books and newspapers are being bought . . . but great dangers reside within prosperity.

The vicar was also angry at the peoples attitude to County Council elections when

only 48% of the population voted. It is not by any means a healthy sign for the community that half the electorate couldn't care less.

The parish remained with a population of just under 3,000, and bearing that figure in mind it was astonishing that a 'rock' service held at one of the big houses, White Craggs, had 2,500 people attending in May 1958! This event was so successful it was repeated for many years. A respondent remembered

they'd get the bishops and the local clergy and there was the Ambleside choir and the Windermere choir . . . one choir would be up on the the big crag and the other would be down on the terrace. It was very theatrical . . . marvellously done. The choir masters looked after it . . . it went on till about 1970 . . .

Is there any end to the quarrels, strikes, lock-outs and wars that we read about everyday? We are so used to these they no longer shock us; we have become immune.

In 1959 the Reverend Bulley, Archdeacon of Westmorland, Director of Religious studies and Vicar of Ambleside and Rydal, was elevated to become a Bishop. Ambleside, he said, 'offered a meagre stipend', as indeed it always had done. Before Mr Bulley left he gave the following statistics:

In 1851 there were about 16,000 clergy, 30% of whom were under 35. In 1951 there were 18,000 clergy and about 10% were under the age of 35, and of course the population had grown significantly over the hundred years. From 1949-1958 4,500 men had been ordained, but 6,000 men had retired or died in that time.

It was said of Mr Bulley that in his time the

choir was always full, a big choir it was lovely . . . If any one was ill connected with the church or even for that matter who didn't come to church very often they always used to visit . . . the Anglicans would stop and have a talk . . . they were much more friendly than the others . . .

The retired Bishop of Penrith took on Ambleside parish as a locum until October 1959 when Mr Warren was appointed. Like Reverend Bulley, Reverend Warren was a man of strong opinions. In 1960 he wrote:

The new age is not a golden age of progress but a 'mushroom' age in which man's complete self-destruction has become a possibility. Humanity seems condemned to live for an indefinite period under the shadow of self-destruction and extinction.

Sharpeville – wholesale slaughter by police – this dreadful and disgraceful act was the consequence of the application of the inhuman doctrine of Apartheid. Nothing can stop the rising tide of Africanisation from claiming for the black man the same basic rights, the same human and political and social rights as the white man.

In 1948 more people emigrated from the United Kingdom than came to live here. Of the immigrants one third were from the Republic of Ireland, and 10% were from the West Indies. The vicar commented on the exodus of the young from Ambleside 'whether they go to University or training college, hospital or elsewhere, they do not return'. The church at this time was running a lively youth club which offered 'rambles, team hunts, barbecues, boat trips, discussions, dancing and games'. He started a midnight Christmas Eve service complete with the choir, and was very pleased to note 218 people came to it.

The Lake District Festival of Music also gained warm approval: in 1962 it went from strength to strength with Andrew Wordsworth reading poetry in Grasmere church, Oxford University Experimental Theatre group put on a revue, and an art exhibition was organised. As part of the festival Ambleside agreed to an orchestral concert in church and 'applause was sanctioned for the first time'.

However, in December 1960 the vicar was preoccupied with the atomic bomb, hurricanes, famine and the 'Berlin Wall of Shame'. Nearer home, he commented that:

one baby in every nine born in London was illegitimate, and in the rest of the country it is about one in twenty. In the borough of Paddington one child in five were born to unmarried mothers.

The other statistic that perturbed him was the rise in drunken driving.

It was the problems caused by hunger that angered him most;

Up till quite recent times Christians could plead ignorance of what went on in the rest of the world: millions might die of famine and nothing be known of it. But now we have no excuse; we know two-thirds of the world are under nourished and one-third in constant hunger. Yet there is enough food in the world for all; it is a problem of distribution.

In June 1962 the Duke of Edinburgh launched a National Freedom from Hunger Campaign. The thrust of the argument was that because 130,000 babies were born everyday, and the world population was now about 3,000 million, the United Nations should take a lead in implementing a programme of advice and aid on contraception. The Duke had support amongst others from Mrs Roosevelt, Dean Acheson, Julian Huxley, Bertrand Russell and Somerset Maugham, but the churches disagreed with this approach.

In October 1962 the second Vatican Council was held in Rome

to try and bridge the gap made by centuries of misunderstanding, misrepresentation and dislike on all sides.

Throughout these years there was a steady increase in prosperity in Ambleside, reflected in the *Home Page* of the magazine which now gave advice on how to clean silver, and how to cook beef provencal. But if housewives were learning to cook with wine, their status in the eyes of the vicar remained the same. The vicar wrote:

the boy going for a job will want prospects with further training, and chance of promotion. For a girl their aim is job satisfaction, money is not important, she will become a wife . . .

The magazine ran articles on racial segregation in the southern states of America, quoting Martin Luther King; it contained vivid letters written from the Missions, and it bewailed the increase of venereal disease, pornography and sexual licence. It showed itself to be acutely aware of the evils of the world, and was keen to promote courses of lectures in Ambleside on 'National and International problems', and 'Man and the Physical World'. But, society was changing rapidly, taboos were being broken down, and the church found it hard to adjust to the realisation that its old authority, or position in society, was gone forever.

In February 1965, Sir Winston Churchill died, and as an epitaph, the vicar gave the following quotation from Churchill's own writings which could be considered to define the man: 'In war resolution, in defeat defiance, in victory magnanimity, and in peace goodwill'. It was the end of an era.

Conclusion

The truism that the history of the parishes is the history of England has considerable validity. Ambleside was a moderately enclosed community up to the time of the second world war, and the vast majority of the population were baptised, educated, married and buried in the parish; the church was pivotal in their lives. The church provided the moral framework and it endorsed the acceptable social activities. Within limits the population was expected to attend a church at least once every Sunday, and by and large it did so.

When the church magazine started in 1879 the church was presented as an authoritarian institution within an authoritarian society; obedience and duty were the key themes. The expectation was that women would have an obedient and dutiful attitude towards their husbands, that children would have an obedient and dutiful attitude towards their parents, and that employees would know their place. The class system was rigid.

The story of the church as reported in the magazine from the 1870s to the 1960s can be interpreted as a story of loss. The erosion by the state into what the church perceived as their provenance as educators of the poor caused anguish. It was not that the church agreed with Cobbett when he questioned the need for a 'ploughboy' to be literate: the church needed a high standard of literacy from children in order that they might pursue their biblical studies. It was a question of control of the school syllabus.

One part of the syllabus the church insisted on was the importance of drill. When the new infants' school was built in Ambleside in 1911 a 'marching corridor' was put down the centre. Learning drill was learning discipline, and it is not too far fetched to suggest that these lessons would be considered invaluable by the Commanders in the field in the first world war, who would rightly expect that when the whistle was blown men would climb out from their trenches to march towards possible death.

The first blow to the authority of the church came in 1907 when Westmorland County Education Department wrote letters to both the girls' school, and the Kelsick boys' school that teachers were no longer to be treated as 'parish workers'. This command had to be complied with because of the threat of the withdrawal of the grant. The crux of the matter was the church had not got the financial ability to go it alone, and they needed the financial aid to bring the schools up to the standard of the council schools or face closure. Although potentially Ambleside had rich patrons, many of them were summer residents, and if they left large legacies they left them elsewhere.

The scholastic expectations for the children was not high, and indeed an argument can be made that after the little Kelsick school was rebuilt to be near the new church of St Mary's, standards fell. The opportunity for boys was radically diminished; no longer were Greek and Latin on the syllabus for seven year olds.

Ambleside at the turn of the twentieth century was a relatively prosperous village because of the availability of domestic employment in the big houses or hotels, but the work could be seasonal. The population never grew significantly because there was a steady migration of the young men who looked for work either elsewhere in Britain or in the Colonies. The Reverend Bayley wrote in 1892 that it seemed to him that

Ambleside, isolated from large towns contains within itself the characteristics of the world in miniature.

Ambleside might be remote from the large industrial cities, but, like them, shared a high mortality rate. It was written in the 1880s in the magazine that 'it was a dark world with death so near'; the infant and childhood mortality rates were high and not only among the poorest of the families. The window in Rydal church commemorates not only Dr and Mrs Arnold but also five of their children who died. In the first forty years after the building of the new churchyard there were 1,164 burials of which no fewer than 341 were for children under the age of ten, by far the largest age group. The 'stinking holes', the dirty contaminated water and tuberculosis led to the high death rate.

Local Government was created at the end of the nineteenth century, and the duly elected councillors believed it was their duty to keep the rates as low as possible. The Council did build a sewage system, they did realise the importance of a clean water supply, and public health inspectors were employed in the field of public health. But it took decades for the Council to come to terms with the proposition that rehousing the poor was part of their responsibilities, and it was not until after the second world war in an era of high taxation that, with intervention from central Government, the substandard housing situation was rectified.

It could be construed that the philosophy of Adam Smith was in full retreat with state intervention into all walks of life with the revolutionary creation of the welfare state. However, later in the twentieth century many council houses were sold off for second homes, and the emphasis again fell on self-help: the Adam Smith Institute remains in a healthy state today.

The church lost the responsibility for the poor before the church magazines started; it lost control of the schools; it lost responsibility for funding the Ambleside commitment to Kendal hospital, and gradually the church began to loose the congregation. However, the greatest loss was the loss of authority. After the second world war society began to change; the role of women changed, the rigid class system changed, and the rules regarding sexual behaviour changed. One of the greatest changes to both church and community was the loss of Sunday as a day apart. Ambleside earned its increasing prosperity from tourism; tourists demanded that the shops and the cafes, like the hotels and the public houses be open seven days a week, and Sunday became the busiest trading day.

Ambleside, the township that built the church for the tourists became subsumed by tourism.

APPENDIX

The Royal Commission on the Endowed Schools of England and Wales

A Special Report on the Endowed Schools of Westmorland

by

D. C. Richmond, Esq.
Assistant Commissioner of the Royal Commission

The report on the Kelsick school in Ambleside is as follows:

There are reasons for hoping that no active steps will be immediately taken towards altering or fixing the present character of the school. The gross annual income is already about £170; nearly half of which is absorbed by the pension enjoyed by the late headmaster since 1848; he is now a very aged man. Besides the sum which will be at disposal after his death, it is probable that in the course of a very few years a large addition will be made to the resources of the school. The permission of the Charity Commissioners has been obtained to the granting of long building leases by which the rent of portions of property in and about the increasing town of Ambleside will be raised to such an extent that, if the whole property to be disposed of be let for building, the annual income of the school will probably amount to at least £400 a year. A few lots have been disposed of, whereby an increase of some £70 has been secured for future years. On this account the Trustees have felt themselves justified in granting a salary of £30 a year to the assistant master who has hitherto been paid chiefly by subscriptions.

The population and wealth of Ambleside are considerable, and a middle class school, for which provision might soon be made out of the the increased revenues of this charity, would be of great value. There seems to be nothing in the founders Will to limit the operation of his benefaction to any one class of inhabitants, whereas the present scholars are mostly of the poorer class. The advantage might hereafter be extended equally to the wealthier people.

The school of course comprises the usual subjects of an elementary education, although under the late headmaster the classics also formed part of the regular work. Drawing has, however lately been introduced and in a few classes book-keeping and mensuration. The writing from dictation of the upper boys aged from 10-15 was very correct, and their arithmetic was well and intelligently done. The first class had attained a very respectable knowledge of English history, and were moderately conversant with geography. Their weakest point was English grammar but this was not very discreditable. In the lower part of the school an unfavourable contrast was presented, the boys being backward and their arithmetic elementary as it was, being purely mechanical. A frequent review by the headmaster of the work done in the lower part of the school would be advantageous.

The behaviour of the boys was orderly; and the large school room which is part of a building lately erected by subscription and in part by a sale of the old school house, affords room for the arrangement of the scholars, who frequently amount to 100 in number. They are chiefly sons of the inhabitants of Ambleside, and no girls are admitted; there are a few scholars from the places who pay a fee which has hitherto formed part of the remuneration made to the assistant master. Scholars from Ambleside pay for their books alone, about which the parents make no difficulty, being, as it appears, well satisfied with the present state of the school.

Balance sheet for 1864/1865

Receipts					*Payments*			
Balance	£	45.	14.	0	Pension to headmaster	£	80.	0.	0
Rents	£	164.	9.	0	Salary to acting H.M.	£	60.	0.	0
Arrears	£	5.	4.	0	Accumulating fund	£	16.	0.	0
					Taxes: Receipts	£	6.	15.	11
					Management	£	5.	7.	4
					Balance	£	47.	3.	9
Total	£	215.	7.	0.	Total	£	215.	7.	0

The object of the Trust is to maintain a master to teach in the free school in Ambleside. In connection with the Church of England, the catechism is taught to all. Daily religious instruction is given and a Sunday school held. There are annual examinations by the incumbent and acting master with no prizes given.

In 1864 there were 84 boys of whom 43 were under the age of 10, and 7 above 14. Out of town boys pay 4s. or 5s. per quarter. The assistant master is paid by subscriptions and by out of town boys.

Mr Richmond was scathing about Kendal.

Kendal is by far the wealthiest and most important town in Westmorland, and the only place that can be called a town. It is the most conspicuous failure. Although there is a remarkable demand still for Latin and Greek in this neighbourhood the Kendal grammar school does next to nothing to meet it and what it does it does badly . . . the general aspect of the school is suggestive of neglect and decay . . . The occupation of parents are shoemakers, bobbin manufacturers, watchmakers, farmers, wallers, carters, tailors and servants.

The Patterdale and Hartsop school was founded in 1766 for a population of 693, with an endowment income of about £5 per annum; the master occupied rooms above the school, and the charges were 4s. or 5s. or 6s. per quarter. Religious instruction was given daily, with prayers before and after school, and there was compulsory Sunday school. The occupation of parents were mining and agriculture.

The Troutbeck school was started in 1639 when it was proscribed that the school master should teach English, Latin and Greek, Writing, and the first four rules of Arithmetic. There is now no demand for classical instruction, and this is simply an elementary school under Government inspection. The school room is low and ill ventilated and not large enough for the 50 to 60 children. There are now only two pupils above the age of 12. The scholars knew no history, but a few had learnt grammar with success.

The school in Bowness

was the object of a very liberal treatment; the present school was erected in 1837 by a Mr J. Bolton. A police station having been built by subscription of the inhabitants of Bowness the annual rent of £10 is allowed to accrue to school funds.

Mr Braithwaite in 1854 left £1,000 to each of four schools in the neighbourhood; this school became entitled to £2,000 for the founding of an exhibition to St John's College, Cambridge. So far no exhibitioner has been appointed.

The school is purely an elementary school for poor children and the wealthier inhabitants send their sons out of Bowness for education. There are 65 scholars, but only 10 girls: there are five scholars between the ages of 11 and 15 who are learning Latin, but only one shows signs of progress. It is to be hoped the upper classes may use the school.

The headmaster who is from the University of London gets £85 per annum, and the second master £60. Children on admission have to be able to read words of two syllables. Prayers are held morning and evening from the Prayer Book and Sunday school is regularly held. Punishment by caning on the hand in public by the headmaster only. The parents include inn keepers, artists, cobblers and farmers.

The annual income from the endowment of Grasmere school in 1866 was £14. 66s. 9d. Under the terms of the endowment there are five free scholars and fifteen who pay only half fees, and the rest pay a quarterage of 4s. The Trustees are the Rector and the sidesmen. The school was built in 1685 and rebuilt in 1854. The object of the Trust is to educated five poor children to be chosen from the industrious poor residents of Grasmere by the Rector and the sidesmen. The school now has 50 boys and girls. The result of the examinations in Arithmetic, Dictation and Geography was very satisfactory; of English grammar and History their knowledge was but small. There were six boys learning mensuration, but there was no recollection of the time when classics were taught. The teacher was certificated.

The Reverend James Simpson, Vicar of Kirby Stephen gave evidence to the Royal Commission. Lord Taunton, for the Commission asked Reverend

Simpson 'What in your opinion is the general character of the endowed schools?' Mr Simpson replied:

With some exceptions I should consider that they are not doing the work they were intended to do. Thirty or forty years ago they were remarkably good, and the reason they have changed is because the condition of the people have changed. Labour has become more valuable, and the cost of living greater; children are so much more valuable to the farmer than they used to be on account of the rise in wages, and again there has been considerable change in the position of the clergy. Another reason is the school master is not so efficient as he used to be. Yeomen were in the habit of educating their sons until the age of 17 or 18, but now land is in fewer hands, young men are more valuable, and farmers cannot afford to keep their sons unemployed. Some younger sons learnt Greek and Latin, and many went into the church and many school masters were clergymen.

Reverend Simpson urged annual inspection of schools, and the

bad school masters should be removed after two poor reports. There were 58-60 endowed schools in Westmorland, the least populated county in England after Rutland, and there were no less than 158 schools in the Diocese of Carlisle.

Lord Lyttleton made another point to the Commission regarding the change of circumstance of the clergy. At the beginning of the nineteenth century the better livings in Westmorland were often held by men who had other livings. They employed curates, did not pay them high stipends, and the curates supplemented their income by teaching. By 1860 better conditions were in place for the clergy, and most parsons did not have to teach to make a living, so the the improvement in the condition of the clergy had a detrimental effect on the schools.

The remedy offered by Mr Simpson was to

make a clear classification of schools between those schools that are intended to educate the middle classes and schools that are simply educating the poor and the children of small farmers . . . who do not require a much better education. It is only the largest farmers and more respectable tradesmen that need education for their children and a higher class of school.

Mr Simpson noted that in the seventeenth century the sons of the gentry went to the local schools, and he quoted the sons of Sir John Lowther,

but now they send their children south by means of railroad.

Simpson also made the point that

there are now far fewer going to Oxford. In 1866 no candidates from Westmorland were sufficiently well prepared to take any one of the four scholarships vacant at Oxford.

Mr Simpson also made the point that endowments were variable, from £7 per annum to £280 per annum with the average endowment of £31. The money from the endowment paid the school master's salary leaving the school often in a poor state of repair and with 'great want of apparatus'. He continued

I have no hesitation in saying that in all cases whatever may be the rank in life there should be payment required from the scholars, and the schools should belong to the Church of England.

When Mr Richmond made his submission to the Royal Commission he said of the Westmorland Statesmen they

did not want the gentility of boarding schools for their sons, but they wanted the village school master to be able to teach them Latin and Greek and to prepare them to go into the church.

It appears to have been regarded almost as a matter of course in the statesmens family that one of the younger sons would become a clergyman.

He would take charge of some mountain township in which the landowners elect their own curate and there he would become schoolmaster as well as perpetuate the learning which has been his own passport into the church.

The village school used to have the function of being both an elementary school, and a finishing school for the gentry. But there have been large changes in reference to the tenure of land with many small owners disappearing and large proprietors taking the place of the statesmen, and there were now a race of poor tenant farmers, some of whom had to find rents of £70 per year.

To reintroduce classical instruction into the small townships or to make their schools in any sense secondary would be vain for the endowments are small, and the pupils too few and the parents too poor to make such schools self supporting. There is no longer sufficient demand to support 40 Grammar schools in Westmorland. But at Bowness and Ambleside the population is to a great extent of comparatively recent origin and is rapidly increasing and the annual incursion of visitors and tourists adds greatly to their wealth. In each of them a secondary school has become a desideratum. Ambleside needs its endowments to be thoroughly reorganised to create a secondary or central school. Special privilege might be reserved for the inhabitants of the central school, and the tributary schools would be like the unendowed National schools and cease to be funded by endowment but would claim Government grants.

The central school would secure a master qualified to teach Latin, Greek, Algebra, Euclid and perhaps higher mathematical subjects and instruction in French should be provided. In the purely agricultural districts instruction in Latin, Algebra, Euclid, mensuration and book-keeping besides the usual English subjects would probably be sufficient.

Mr Richmond concluded his submission to the Royal Commission by saying that in his opinion

the spirit of honourable ambition which prevails among the youth of the lower middle class in this country must be encouraged . . . a promising boy of parentage however poor might rise first from the small primary school to the nearest central school and may be passed on as an exhibitioner to a public school of the highest class . . .

Bibliography

Armitt, Mary. *Ambleside Town and Chapel*. Published 1906. Titus Wilson, Kendal.

Bingham, Roger. *Kendal. A Social History*. Published 1990. Cicerone Press, Milnthorpe, England.

Bouch, Canon C. M. and G. P. Jones, D.Litt. *A Short Economic and Social History of the Lake Counties 1500-1830*. Published 1961. University of Manchester.

Chadwick, Owen. *History of the Victorian Church, Vol 1 and Vol 2*. Published 1970. Adam and Charles Black.

Cholmondeley, Essex. *The Story of Charlotte Mason*. Published 1960. J. M. Dent and Sons, Aldine Press, Bedford Street, London.

Clough, Blanche Athena. *Memoir of Anne J. Clough*. Published 1897. Arnold, London.

Cruikshank, Marjorie. *Church and State in English Education 1870 to the Present Day*. Published 1963. Macmillan.

Derry and Jarman. *The Making of Modern Britain*. Published 1971. John Murray Publishers Ltd., 50 Albemarle Street, London W1X 4BD.

Harwood, Sir John James. *History and Description of the Thirlemere Water Scheme*. Published 1895. Blacklock and Co.

Jay, Eileen. *The Armitt Story*. Published 1998. The Loughrigg Press, Ambleside.

Marshall and Walton. *The Lakes Counties from 1830 to the mid-twentieth Century*. Published 1981. Manchester University Press, Oxford Road, Manchester M13 9PL.

Martineau, Harriet. *Autobiography*. First Published 1877. Reproduced 1983. Virago Press.

Moorman, J. R. H., M.A., D.D. *History of the Church in England*. Published 1953. A. & C. Black Ltd. 4, 5, 6 Soho Square, London W.1.

Nicholson, Norman. *The Lake District. An Anthology*. Published 1977. Robert Hale Ltd.

Slater, Gilbert. *The Growth of Modern England*. Published 1932. Constable and Co. Ltd.

Somervell, Robert. *Protest against Extention of the Railway in the Lake District*. Preface by John Ruskin. Published 1887.

Scott, Joe. (ed.). *A Lakeland Valley Through Time*. Published 1995. Stavely and District History Society.

Taylor, A. J. P. *English History 1914-1945*. Published 1965. Oxford University Press, Penguin Books Ltd, Harmsworth, Middlesex, England.

Tyler, Ian. *Thirlemere Mines and the Drowning of the Valley*. Published 1998. Blue Rock Publications, Thirlemere Mining Museum, Threlkeld Quarry, Keswick, Cumbria CA12 4TT.

Wheatley, Vera. *The Life and Work of Harriet Martineau*. Published 1957. Secker and Warburg, 7 John St., London W.C.1.

Watson, John. *Annuals of a Quiet Valley in the Wordsworth Country*. Published 1895. J. M. Dent.

Watson, Kathy. *History of Ambleside*. 1979. Thesis deposited Armitt Library.

Directories

Parson and White. *Directory of Cumberland and Westmorland.* Published 1829.

Mannex and Co. *Directory of Westmorland with Lonsdale and Amounderness in Lancashire.* Published 1851.

Kellys Directory of Cumberland and Westmorland. Published 1897.

Kellys Directory of Westmorland. Published 1934.

Cumbrian Record Office:

Minutes of Girls and Infants National School 1877-1918.

Minutes of Ambleside Urban District Council 1885-1935.

Minutes of Lakes Urban Disrict Council 1935-1965.

Notes deposited by the Reverend Charles Chase.

Evidence of the Reverend James Simpson given to the Royal Commission on the Endowed Schools of Westmorland 1866.

Special Report by P. C. Richmond. Schools Enquiry Commission, Vol. xix. Northern Division.

Kelsick Papers. The Kelsick Trust.

The Church Magazines 1879-1965. The Armitt Library.

Endnotes

CHAPTER ONE

'Be Earnest! Be Earnest!'

Page

2   'Poor Man's Robbery Act . . .'. William Cobbett. Quoted by Owen Chadwick. *History of the Victorian Church*, Vol. 1, p. 96.

2   'Lord Shafesbury the noblest . . .'. Owen Chadwick. *History of the Victorian Church*, Vol. 1, p. 463.

3   In 1830 it was a matter . . .'. Owen Chadwick. *History of the Victorian Church*. Vol. 1, p. 518.

3   'Mid-Victorian England was . . .'. J. R. H. Moorman. *History of the Church in England*, p. 390.

3   'of an old circular . . .'. Reverend Charles Chase. Cumbria Record Office.

4   'Shout Loughrigg from . . .'. Reverend Charles Chase. Cumbria Records Office.

4   'It is a serious matter . . .'. Harriet Martineau, *Autobiography*. p. 306.

4   'discontent in the parish . . .'. Harriet Martineau, *Autobiography*. p. 302.

4   'In the church here . . .'. Quoted *Church Magazine*. 1957.

5   'coaches run frantically . . .'. Harriet Martineau, p. 267.

5   'the town has a modern aspect . . .'. Parson and Whites. *Directory of Cumberland and Westmortland*, 1829.

5   'two small cannons are kept . . .'. Mannex and Co. *Directory of Westmorland*, 1851.

5   'proposed to allow . . .'. Letter from William Wordsworth. Armitt Library.

5   'We have no fear . . .'. Martineau on 'The Coming of the Railway', Quoted by Norman Nicholson, *The Lake District*, p. 220.

6   'tourism to the Lakes . . .'. Marshall and Walton. *The Lake Counties*, p. 63.

6   'It has proved a great . . .'. *Church Magazine*, 1879.

6   'I am hoping . . .'. *Church Magazine*, 1879.

7   'drink affected not only . . .'. *Church Magazine*, 1879.

7   'unfortunately marred . . .'. *Church Magazine*, 1879.

7   'a simple and refreshing . . .'. *Church Magazine*, 1879.

7   'pray before voting . . .'. *Church Magazine*, 1880.

8   'A Sunday Closing Bill . . .'. *Church Magazine*, 1880.

8   'When people are compelled. . . .'. Harriet Martineau *Autobiography*, p. 306.

8   'coloured prints used . . .'. Harriet Martineau *Autobiography*, p. 309.

8   'an abomination in all . . .'. Letter to Lord Morpeth from Harriet Martineau, 1848. Armitt Library.

8   'heaven helps those . . .'. Samuel Smiles. 1859. Quoted in *Nature and Industrialisation*. Ed. Alasdair Clayre.

Page

9   'all who can should . . .'. *Church Magazine*, 1881.

9   'they only help the deserving . . .'. *Church Magazine*, 1881.

10 'Whitsuntide is the season . . .'. *Church Magazine*, 1880.

10 'disorderly conduct on Lake Road . . .'. *Church Magazine*, 1880.

10 'Be Earnest! Be Earnest! *Church Magazine*, 1880.

10 'Parents must insist . . .'. *Church Magazine*, 1881.

10 'I am desirous . . .'. *Church Magazine*, 1881.

11 'Why should you teach . . .'. William Cobbett. Quoted by Owen Chadwick. *History of the Victorian Church*, p. 337.

11 'The School room near . . .'. Report from the Charity Commissioners 1815.

12 'The position of the teacher . . .' . *Memoirs of Anne Clough* by her niece Blanche Athena Clough, p. 88.

13 'parents do not like . . .'. *Memoirs of Anne Clough*, p. 87.

13 'I am delighted. . . .'. Harriet Martineau. Letter to Richard Moncton Milnes, 1843. Armitt Library.

14. 'To reintroduce classical instruction . . .'. from evidence given to the Royal Commission on Endowed Schools 1864. D. C. Richmond.

15 'I was in want . . .'. Quoted in *Church Magazine*, 1957.

16. 'In consequence of . . .'. Minute book *Girls' and Infants' National School*. Cumbria Record Office.

16 'Owing to the rise . . .'. Minute book *Girls' and Infants' National School*. Cumbria Record Office.

17. 'to obtain complete . . .'. *Church and State in English Education*. Marjorie Cruikshank, p. 22.

17 'entail upon the country . . .'. *Church and State in English Education*. Marjorie Cruikshank p. 22.

18 'average expenditure . . .'. *Church and State in English Education*. Marjorie Cruikshank p. 55.

18 'a school rate . . .'. *Church Magazine*, 1891.

19 'The estimated population . . .'. *Church Magazine*, 1890.

19 'Our interest in . . .'. *Church Magazine*, 1890.

19 'by the end of . . .'. *History of the Victorian Church*, Vol. 2, Owen Chadwick, p. 24.

19 'I wish we could . . .'. *Church Magazine*, 1888.

20 'There is one request . . .'. *Church Magazine*, 1882.

20 'We live in days . . .'. *Church Magazine*, 1882.

20 'Temperance tea . . .'. *Church Magazine*, 1882.

20 'We are anxious . . .'. *Church Magazine*, 1885.

21 'he could only wonder . . .'. *Church Magazine*, 1884.

21 'to be honest, pure . . .'. *Church Magazine*, 1885.

21 'times were hard . . .'. *Church Magazine*, 1885.

22 'dire distress . . .'. *Church Magazine*, 1885.

22 'that although . . .'. *History of the Victorian Church*, Vol. 2. Owen Chadwick p. 167.

22 'Some of our neighbours . . .'. *Church Magazine*.

23 'For months . . .'. *Thirlmere Mines and the Drowning of the Valley*. Ian Tyler, p. 158.

24 'there was a work force . . .'. *Thirlmere Mines and the Drowning of the Valley*. Ian Tyler, p. 158.

CHAPTER TWO

'Blessed by Drudgery'

CHAPTER THREE

'Reader Pause and Think!'

CHAPTER FOUR

'Great Dangers Reside within Prosperity'

Page

107 'Forty years ago . . .'. *Church Magazine*. 1946.

108 'There are two urgent . . .'. *Church Magazine*. 1946.

108 'Diocese of Southwark . . .'. *Church Magazine*. 1946.

108 'which will cost . . .'. *Church Magazine*. 1946.

108 'we are still suffering . . .'. *Church Magazine*. 1946.

108 'we must cleanse . . .'. *Church Magazine*. 1947.

108 'in 1855 . . .'. Report by Lord Justice Denning Master of the Rolls, quoted in the *Church Magazine*, 1947.

109 'Is England a Christian Country? . . .'. *Church Magazine*. 1947.

109 'dedication of the tablet . . .'. *Church Magazine*. 1947.

109 'in which he gave . . .'. *Church Magazine*. 1948.

109 'there are no depths . . .'. *Church Magazine*. 1948.

109 'Looking back . . .'. Winston Churchill. 'The Gathering Storm' quoted in *Church Magazine*, 1948.

110 'Thee are two powers . . .'. *Church Magazine*. 1948.

110 'local people must take . . .'. *Church Magazine*. 1950.

111 'grave words . . .'. *Church Magazine*. 1951.

111 'back to evangelism . . .'. *Church Magazine*. 1951.

111 'It is not . . .'. *Church Magazine*. 1952.

111 'Broadly speaking . . .'. *Church Magazine*. 1952.

111 'Convictions for drunkenness . . .'. *Church Magazine*. 1952.

111 'millions of refugees . . .'. *Church Magazine*. 1950.

112 'The decline in sanctions . . .'. *Church Magazine*. 1953.

113 'There were these toilets . . .'. Ambleside Oral History Group.

113 'will probably mean . . .'. *Church Magazine*. 1943.

113 'Some of the Country . . .'. *Church Magazine*. 1946.

114 'This plan will . . .'. *Church Magazine*. 1946.

114 'following the 1944 . . .'. *Church Magazine*. 1948.

115 'The diocese is . . .'. *Church Magazine*. 1950.

115 'Their purposes . . .'. *Church Magazine*. 1957.

115 'The Infants' School . . .'. *Church Magazine*. 1959.

115 'Kelsick School . . .'. *Church Magazine*. 1959.

115 'The Comprehensive school . . .'. *Church Magazine*. 1957.

115 'its primary purpose . . .'. *Church Magazine*. 1959.

116 'Before the war . . .'. Ambleside Oral History Group.

116 'The decision to . . .'. *Church Magazine*. 1960.

116 'In January . . .'. *Church Magazine*. 1961.

116 'it is the intention . . .'. *Church Magazine*. 1959.

117 'How to Salvage . . .'. Minutes, Lakes Urban District Council.

119 'if they were considering . . .'. Minutes, Lakes Urban District Council.

119 'extensive works with . . .'. Minutes, Lakes Urban District Council.

119 'The need for automatic . . .'. Minutes, Lakes Urban District Council.

119 'had a head start . . .'. Ambleside Oral History Group.

119 'to request the Council . . .'. Minutes, Lakes Urban District Council.

120 'Whereas it has . . .'. Minutes, Lakes Urban District Council.

120 'provision was made . . .'. Minutes, Lakes Urban District Council.

Page

120 'increasing problems . . .'. Minutes, Lakes Urban District Council.

120 'there were all sorts . . .'. Ambleside Oral History Group.

121 'formal objection . . .'. Lakes Urban District Council.

121 'over the world . . .'. *Church Magazine*. 1954.

121 'Christian people . . .'. *Church Magazine*. 1954.

122 'Public Opinion . . .'. Lord Justice Denning, Master of the Rolls quoted in the *Church Magazine*, 1954.

122 'Conflict of the day . . .'. *Church Magazine*. 1954.

122 'Addiction to alcohol . . .'. *Church Magazine*. 1955.

122 '90% of all . . .'. *Church Magazine*. 1956.

122 'although Ambleside was . . .'. *Church Magazine*. 1956.

123 'In 1956 . . .'. *Church Magazine*. 1956.

123 'The flags of all . . .'. *Church Magazine*. 1956.

123 'The massacre . . .'. *Church Magazine*. 1956.

123 'There is no clear . . .'. *Church Magazine*. 1957.

124 'People are better . . .'. *Church Magazine*. 1962.

124 'only 48% . . .'. *Church Magazine*. 1962.

124 'they'd get the Bishops . . .'. Ambleside Oral History Group.

124 'Is there any . . .'. *Church Magazine*. 1959.

124 'In 1851 . . .'. *Church Magazine*. 1959.

124 'choir was always . . .'. Ambleside Oral History Group.

124 'the new age . . .'. *Church Magazine*. 1960.

125 'one baby in . . .'. *Church Magazine*. 1960.

125 'up till quite recently . . .'. *Church Magazine*. 1961.

126 'to try and . . .'. *Church Magazine*. 1961.

126 'the boy going . . .'. *Church Magazine*. 1962.

Index